Hawaii
from the air

WHITE STAR
PUBLISHERS

CONTENTS

Photographs
Antonio Attini

Text
Erin Mc Closkey

Captions
Enrico Lavagno

Graphic Design
Paola Piacco

© 2003 White Star S.r.l.
Via C. Sassone, 22/24
13100 Vercelli, Italy
www.whitestar.it

TRANSLATION OF THE CAPTIONS
Amy Christine Ezrin

ISBN 88-540-0014-0

Reprints:
1 2 3 4 5 6   07 06 05 04 03

Printed in Korea
Color separation by Fotomec - Turin

1 In one of the remotest places on the planet, where land and sea create a perfect union, the Hawaiian Islands reveals their unique natural splendor.

2-3 The cliffs of the Na Pali Coast, on Kauai's the north coast rise 4000 feet above the crest of the waves.

4-5 Waimea Canyon, the "Grand Canyon of the Pacific," cuts deeply into the western portion of Kauai.

6 Thin as a thread, a waterfall tumbles down from the sheer Waialelale Crater on Kauai.

7 Nero with lava, the coast of Big Island at the base of Kilauea continues to grow without rest, fed by the volcano's incessant activity.

8-9 Although bold, the Honolulu skyline cannot compete with the magnificence of Diamond Head.

10-11 Tiny Molokai lighthouse stands proud on Kahiu Point, the island's northernmost point.

12-13 The impressive waves that roll onto Hawaii's shores are a surfer's dream, but sometimes run so high that it's dangerous to stay on the beach.

Aloha may be what comes closest to expressing the spirituality that visitors feel when experiencing the undeniable beauty of the Hawaiian Islands. Aloha means more than "hello"; when spoken, it is in recognition of the presence of the divine.

Indeed, the gods must smile down upon this paradise of lush impenetrable rainforests, deep exotic valleys, awesome and forbidding mountains and craggy cliffs. To fly above the valleys speck-led with little villages and checkered with green taro fields is enchanting. To soar above the rain-forest canopies of dense wet greenery and massive volcanic craters is inspiring. To gaze upon the islands from above gives the sense of communing with the pantheon of Hawaiian gods. The chants of the ancient chiefs are still carried in the winds and the faces of warrior spirits seem profiled in the sheer walls of stone that rise up from the massive canyons and cast their austere

The dichotomy of the islands is the perpetual feud that seems to be running between the elements of fire and water. Charred black terrain is buttressed against lush tropical greens. Red-hot eruptions of volcanic lava char and burn the terrain black but are countered by the tropical moisture-storing clouds that nourish the landscape with bountiful rains that quench the charred earth and fill the rivers.

Waterfalls that tumble from virtually every cliff and from the summits of massive craters are born in rebellious snowcaps and glaciers. Lava streams down mountainsides to arrive at the ocean whose defiant white lashing waves beat it back into submission. Underwater magma bursts from the Hawaiian "hot spot" that remains uncooled by the bountiful blues of the Pacific. Fantastic explosive scenes of erupting molten lava fire the imagination, yet so much of the Hawaiian Islands is tropically wet and humid, characterized by water. Rainforests abound with giant ferns that poke up through the leaves and fronds of the treetops like sea-green anemones, and lacy white waterfalls hang from cliffs like flimsy négligées or pour like champagne bursting and bubbling from a freshly opened bottle.

The dramatic birth of the archipelago occurred only a mere 25 to 40 million years ago when hot magma burst a fissure through the ocean floor; then from the fiery molten core of the earth it burped and bubbled, pillowed and mounded, and built up into a great mountainous volcano. This giant inched its massive foot off the hot spot to make way for the next of its kin to climb out from the underworld. The Hawaiian Islands have emerged one at a time as the Pacific Plate shifts northwest across the hot spot at a rate of two to three inches per year.

The fires below the Hawaiian hot spot still rage unquenched, conceiving new islands to add to the archipelago. From the fires of volcanic eruptions occurring on the primordial ocean floor, new islands are born while older islands continue to grow from continuous volcanic eruptions, adding acres of land to their mass. This powerful energy of nature is the mana that pulses through the mountains, rivers and valleys throughout the archipelago.

Eighty-two volcanoes form the string of pearls that are in reality the peaks of massive underwater mountains.

gaze toward the horizon. Enormous waves boldly grasp and roll themselves shoreward as if they too would like to flood up onto the inviting beaches to lie on the back and feel the kiss of the Hawaiian sun. This lovely archipelago of islands, islets, coral reefs and atolls is centered on a blue canvas of ocean; he far-flung chain seems to have chosen its location to be as far away as possible from all other continents; they seem to radiate around it at a respectful distance, miles and miles away.

14 Oahu (left, northwesterly) and Maui (right), right in this fine aerial shot taken from the northwest, begins the main Hawaiian archipelago.

15 Kauai, bottom left in this view of the Hawaiian archipelago, with Molokai, Lanai, and Kahoolawe in the center.

INTRODUCTION

and active as some of the Hawaiian volcanoes are, most can be approached almost to the summit. A brilliant bird's-eye view of an erupting volcano is an unforgettable experience. The calderas of some volcanoes churn with boiling red lava, steaming with biting fumes of sulfur and chlo-

of lava bursting like a geyser from the crater and then traveling down the mountainside, chunky and thick, plowing forward like a massive steaming bulldozer (called Aa-type lava). Or it may be liquid and sinewy, slithering and winding itself along a hot, ropy path (pahoe-

hoe-type lava). Pele, the goddess of fire and volcanoes, whose home is in the heart of Kilauea Volcano, is said to be seen starting out from the flames of fires and in the vibrant splashes of lava, the blast from volcanic eruptions. Glass is formed in shards, or in thin and cobwebby

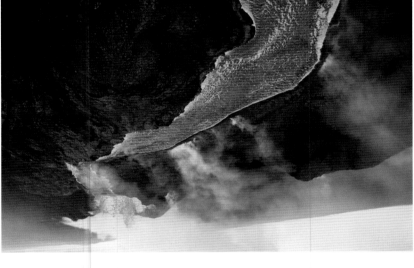

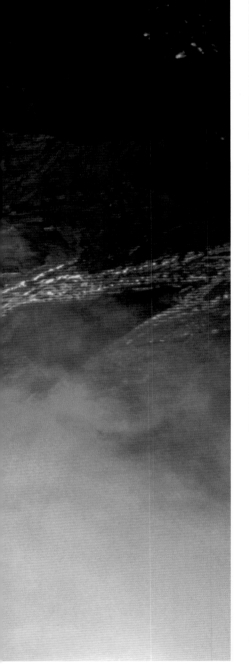

From above an active caldera, a red lava lake may be seen boiling and belching in small eruptions that stay within the cone, while scars from old lava flows often distinctively etch the slopes. A beautiful sight is the lava tube's "skylights," where the ground has caved in and the flowing lava can be seen like a red glowing window. As massive

rine, while a number of extinct volcanoes hold tranquil pools of azure water and still others are stuffed to overflowing with ferns and fronds. Their only eruption may be a burst of red feathers as a startled bird takes flight from the canopy.

Eruptions occur quite frequently at Hawaii Volcanoes National Park, often with a fount

16 top and bottom The ever-percolating Puu O'o, on the slopes of the Big Islands Kilauea volcano, is under constant watch.

16-17 Kilauea is a "secondary" mouth on the wide shallow basin of the crater of Mauna Loa, on Hawaii.

17 top Before flowing out of Puu O'o, the lava has traversed a seven-mile underground starting within Kilauea volcano.

18-19 On Molokai, an amazing series of natural pools connect the waterfalls that pour down in through Kalaupapa National Park.

20-21 A pineapple plantation prospers in the fertile volcanic soil of Oahu. The fruit was probably brought to Hawaii by Polynesians from far-away Tahiti.

strands, by volcanic gasses blowing through the hot air-born lava. This glass is called Pele's tears or Pele's hair, according to its type.

This dramatic beginning and earthshaking geological evolution of the Hawaiian Islands contrasts with one of the planet's slowest and most gentle biological evolutions. Until man first set foot upon Hawaii's volcanic soil only a few hundred years ago, evolution in these remote islands had been a discreet and isolated affair.

Yet, Hawaiian plants and animals remain a treasure trove of unique beauties. The islands enjoy a situation of isolation within isolation: they are separated from the nearest landmass by at least 2,000 miles (2,390 miles from California and 3,850 miles from Japan). The individual islands are separated from each other, and on each island several microclimates exist such as those that differentiate the rainy leeward sides of mountains from the dry windward sides.

Each island is unique, different from the others, and reveals individual charms whose unparalleled splendors intrigue the visitor.

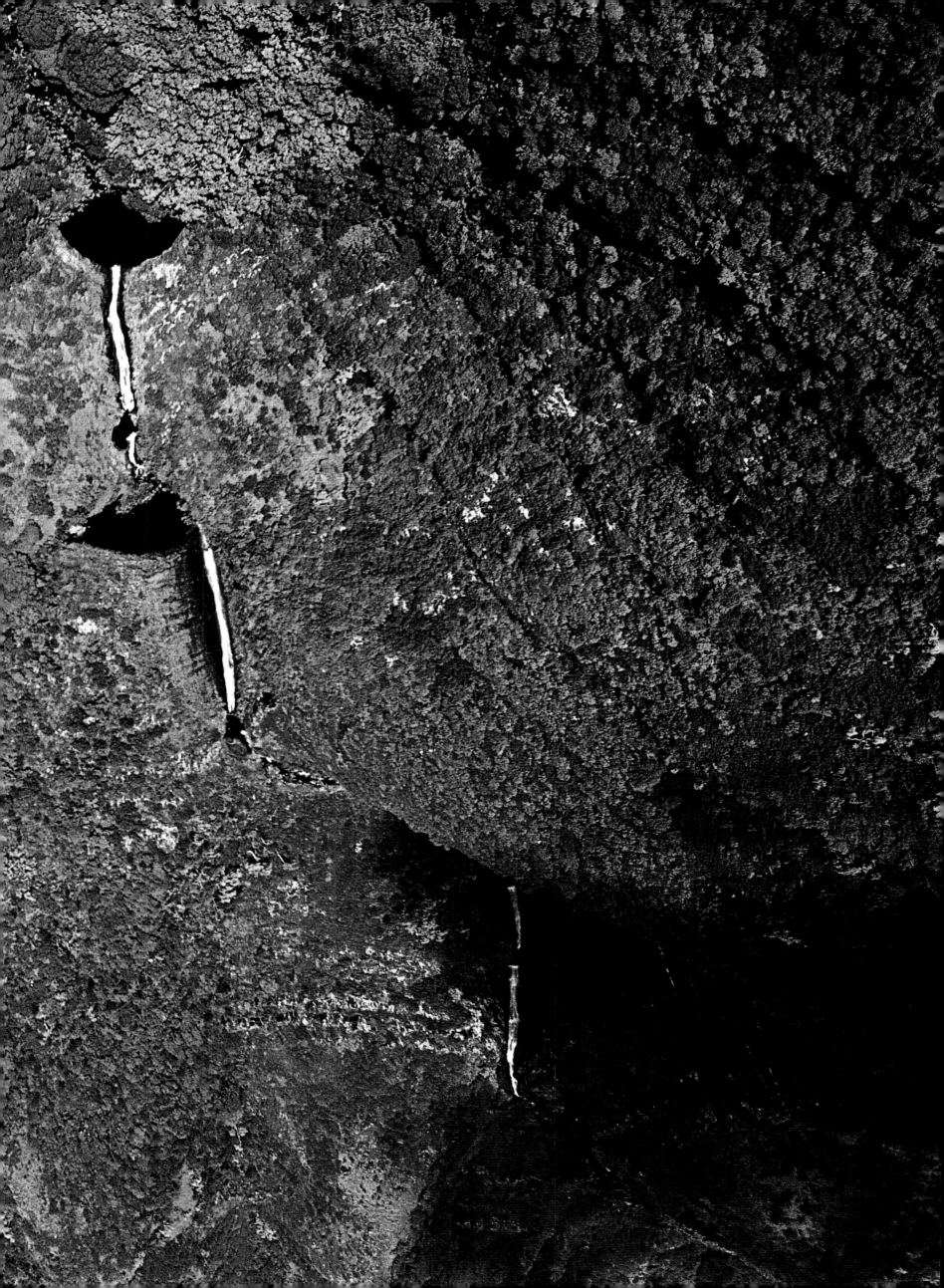

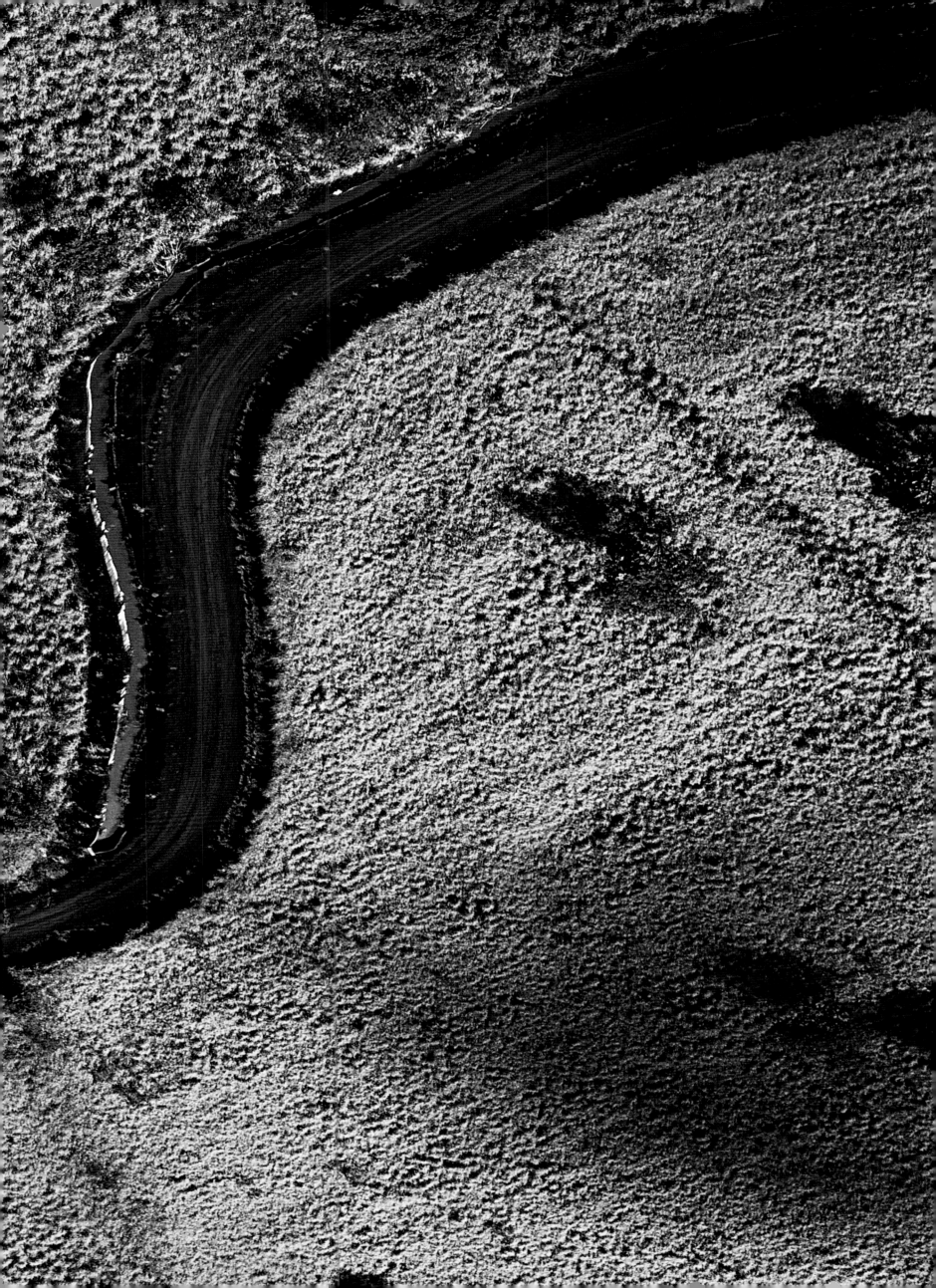

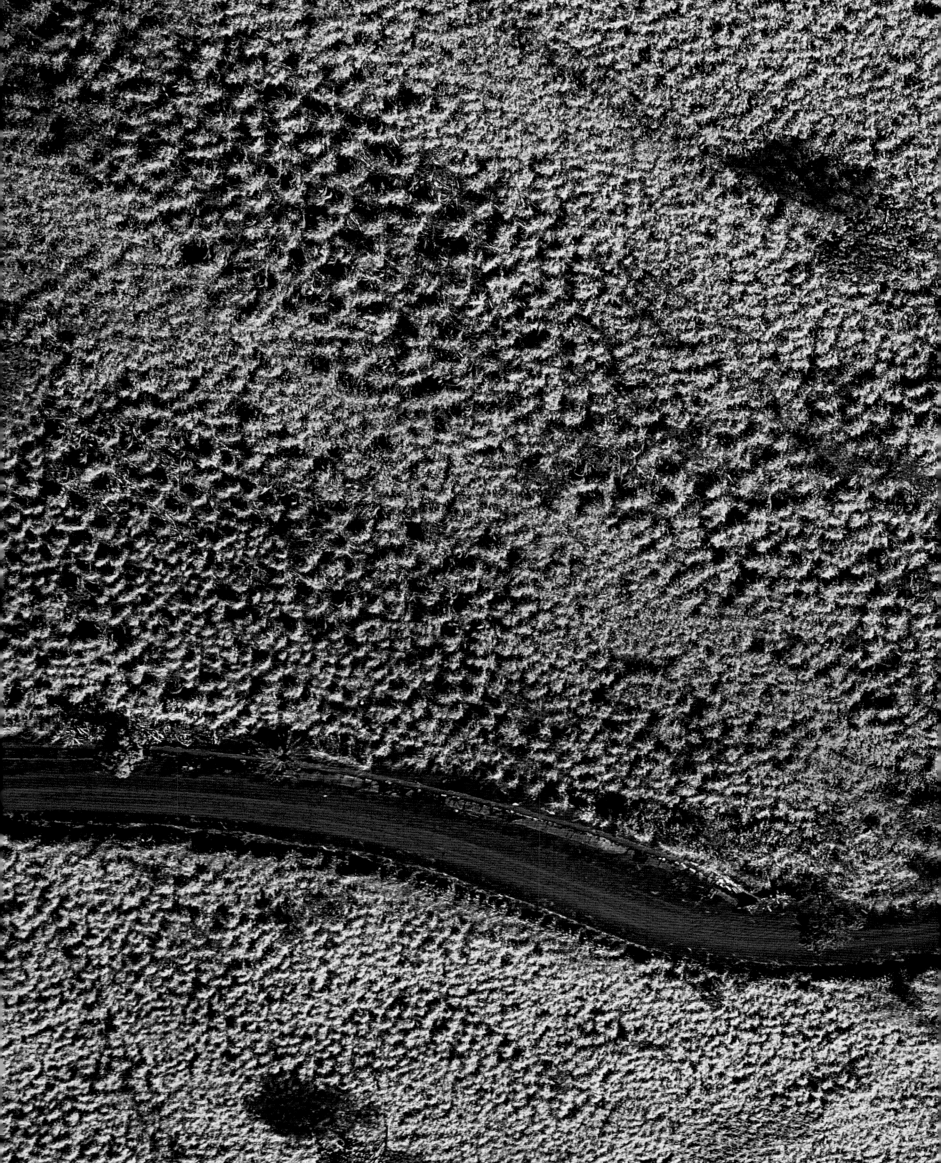

BIG ISLAND

22-23 The slopes of
Kilauea feature
truly "infernal"
landscapes, with
puddles of smoking
lava among a
chaotic jumble of
basaltic rocks.

23 top Lava has
continued to flow
out of Kilauea since
January 1983: since
then, the crater has
added acres of
territory to the
island.

23 bottom The
erupting Puu O'o is
enveloped in steam:
only a few times a
year does this
Kilauea crater limit
itself to emitting
mere puffs of smoke.

T he "Big Island" justifies its name by being not only the archipelago's largest island (all the other islands could fit into just one half of Hawaii's 4,028 square miles) but also as an island character-ized by the awesome grandeur of astounding mountains and volcanoes. In fact, much of this island seems to go out of its way to impress. There are mas-sive waterfalls, great swathes of forest and valley, some 266 miles of coastline, and ancient temples including the Pu-uhonua O Honaunau refuge, surmised to have been founded around 1200 AD. Then there is an abundance of flowers, espe-cially orchids—however, only three native species of orchid are found on the island of Hawaii, which is sometimes called The Orchid Island. Botanical gardens grow several species and varieties of orchids as well as many other tropical flowers such as the fragrant plumeria and the white and yel-low ginger. The flowers are

grown to make the beautiful leis that have become symbolic of Hawaii—along with volcanoes.

Five impressive volcanoes formed the great island of Hawaii: Mauna Kea, Mauna Loa, Kilauea, Hualalai and Kohala. Estimated at a million years old, Mauna Kea is often snow-capped, giving it the look of a wise old ancient wrapped in his ashen cloak and topped with a head of white hair. There is gla-cial ice a few feet below the sur-face—Mauna Kea is the only Hawaiian volcano known to have a glacier. The snow-god-dess Poliahu keeps vigilance from her home on the summit of Puu Poliahu. Legend recounts the ancient and sacred battle be-tween Pele and Poliahu in which Poliahu beat back the fires of Pele with her snowy white cloak. Hibernating be-neath the blanket of winter snowiness, Mauna Kea may one day awaken, shake off its bur-den, open its mouth in a mighty yawn to a proverbial spring, and thaw its frozen flanks.

Mauna Kea is the highest volcano on Earth; if measured from its base on the ocean floor it is 32,976 feet high, taller than Mount Everest. Atop Mauna Kea, at its 13,750-foot summit, is the world's largest observatory for optical, infrared and submillimeter astronomy, known for its twin Keck telescopes. The site was chosen owing to the summit's environment of thermally stable ocean air and lack of nearby mountain ranges and city lights. The atmosphere above Mauna Kea is celebrated for being extremely clear, calm and dry—perfect for stargazing. Also situated at these star-reaching heights is Lake Waiau, located in the Pu'u Waiau Crater. It is the only permanent body of water on Mauna Kea and is the world's highest alpine lake. The ancient Hawaiians believed it to be the bottomless and the portal to the underworld; here they would make offerings of newborn children to the god, so that their other children would be blessed with long, healthy lives.

The true fiery glory of the island is Hawaii Volcanoes National Park. The park is a UNESCO World Heritage Site and is the abode of two grumbling giants: Kilauea and Mauna Loa volcanoes. The latter and larger of the two, Mauna Loa volcano is slumbering for the time being but it does awaken occasionally; the eruption in 1984 lasted 22 days. At 13, 680 feet above sea level, 19,000 cubic miles in volume and covering an area of 2,035 square miles (roughly half of the entire island of Hawaii), Mauna Loa is the most massive mountain on Earth. Though at present slumbering peacefully, Mauna Loa has had a restless period in the last century, when it erupted on average every 3.8 years. A great eruption in 1950 produced such an abundant volume of lava that it is said to have been sufficient for paving a four-lane highway four-and-one-half-times around the earth!

Kilauea is the youngest volcano on the island of Hawaii but is also one of the world's most active. Topographically it appears as no more than a bulge on Mauna Loa's southeastern flank, and for many years cartographers did not consider it to be a separate volcano. It does, however, have an independent magma source going more than 35 miles deep into the earth. Kilauea has been in a state of constant eruption since 1983, when it burst forth with a 40-foot fountain of lava. The current eruption phase has already lasted for over 20 years, and geologists theorize that the activity could continue for several more. It is also the island's most voluminous volcano in recorded history, spewing 250,000 to 650,000 cubic yards of lava per day and having added 500 acres to the island in the past 12 years. Kilauea has given the island a stunning topography of craters, pits, lava tubes, lava deserts and elegant black sand beaches, such as those at Kaimu, Punalu'u and Kahalu'u. The volcano offers spectacular shows when the crimson lava bursts from the crater and burns its molten path through swaths of tropical greenery to arrive steaming at the Pacific shore, where the waters seem to push back with a determined counterforce. Though undeniably beautiful, Kilauea is also highly destructive. It has covered 16,000 lowland acres in as much as 80 feet of lava, and has destroyed large areas of rainforests as well as towns and villages. The Pu'u 'O'o eruption of Kilauea has had over 35 episodes of vigorous activity characterized by spectacular lava fountains that have catapulted lava as high as 1,500 feet above the vent. The eruptions of Pu'u 'O'o-Kupaianaha claimed the Waha'ula Visitor Center of Hawaii Volcanoes National Park in 1989 and, in the following year, the entire town of Kalapana, with its valuable historic sites and dozens of homes, was destroyed.

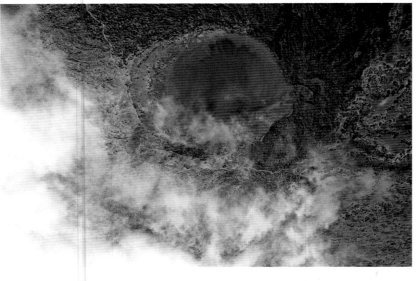

24 top *The buildings of the Mauna Kea Observatory are silhouetted against the horizon. The site was chosen for the ocean air's frequent high-clarity readings.*

24 bottom *The Mauna Kea craters are the legendary dwelling place of Poliahu, the goddess of snow who makes crystal tears shed for lost lovers fall from the sky.*

25 *Spines of burned rock emerge in the area of Mauna Loa, creating highly fascinating environments. The volcano is still active, though eruptions are rare.*

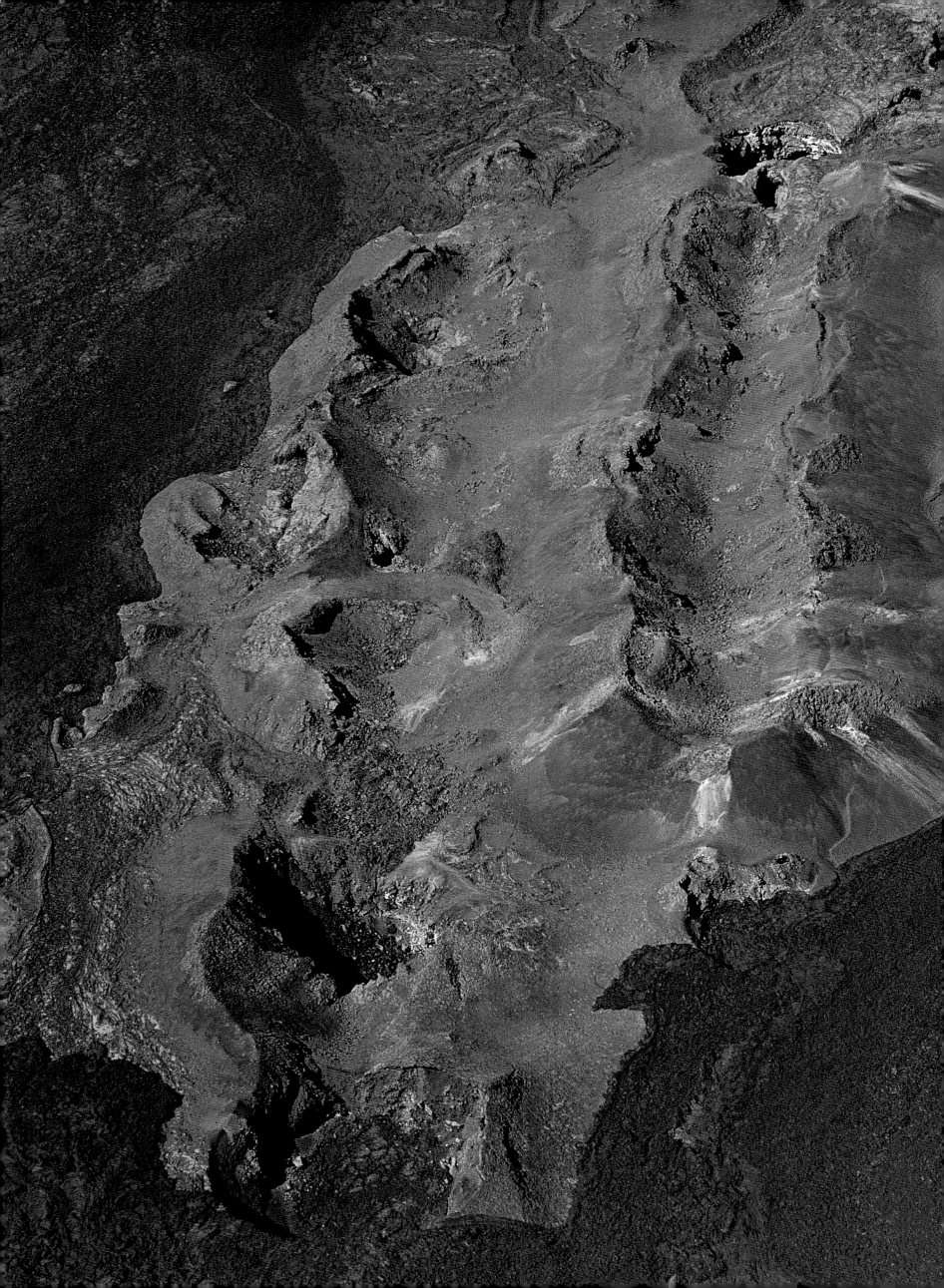

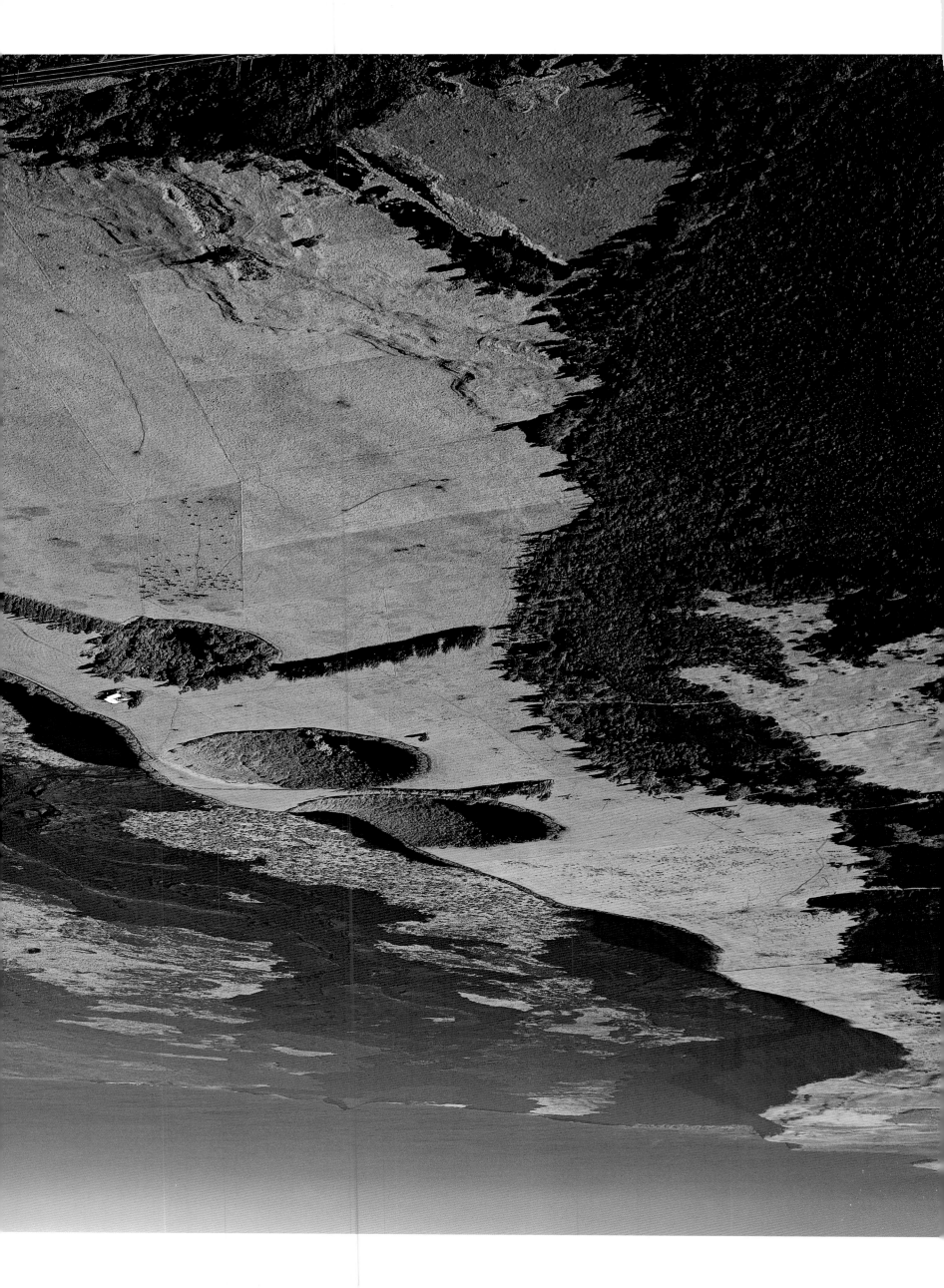

Prior to Kilauea's current eruption phase there have been several significant previous ones. Still visible are the ashen foot-prints of Chief Keoau's one hundred warriors, on their way to battle against Kamehameha in 1790 when they were ambushed by an unexpected foe—the lavas of Kilauea, in a massive eruption. There was also a significant erup-tion back in 1924. More recently, two large events occurred in the 1950s; in one, lava shot out and poured from Kilauea for 88 days and destroyed Pahoa village.

steams in exhaustion.

Kilauea is the legendary home of the fire goddess Pele, creator of the molten fountains, the melter of rocks, the builder of moun-tains, the eater of forests, the burner of lands and the governor of the great lava flows. Her ghost-ly long-haired image is some-times believed to be seen in pho-tographs of the eruptions. She is the daughter of Haumea, the Earth Mother, and Wakea, the Sky Father, and she embodies the paradoxical roles of both creator and destroyer.

Kupaianaha collapsed upon itself in 1992, but Pu'u 'O'o is still active and unpredictable. The oval rim around the sum-mit of the Kilauea caldera is 2.5 miles across and 300 feet deep. Surrounding the caldera are the Iki, Kenakakoi and Halema'u-ma'u craters. The last of these three, called Halema'uma'u, or "The Fire Pit," is in the central part of the pan. Here a lava lake could at one time be seen from above, stewing and boiling, but it has collapsed upon itself and now only smokes and

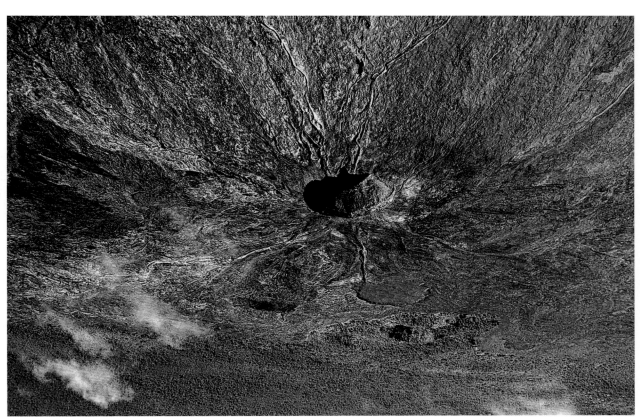

26-27 The craters of long-dead volcanoes mark the edges of a plateau in Hawaii Volcanoes National Park.

streams of black lava are called kipuka.

27 top "Islands" of green spared by vegetation.

27 bottom A relatively recent cone has developed amid vegetation.

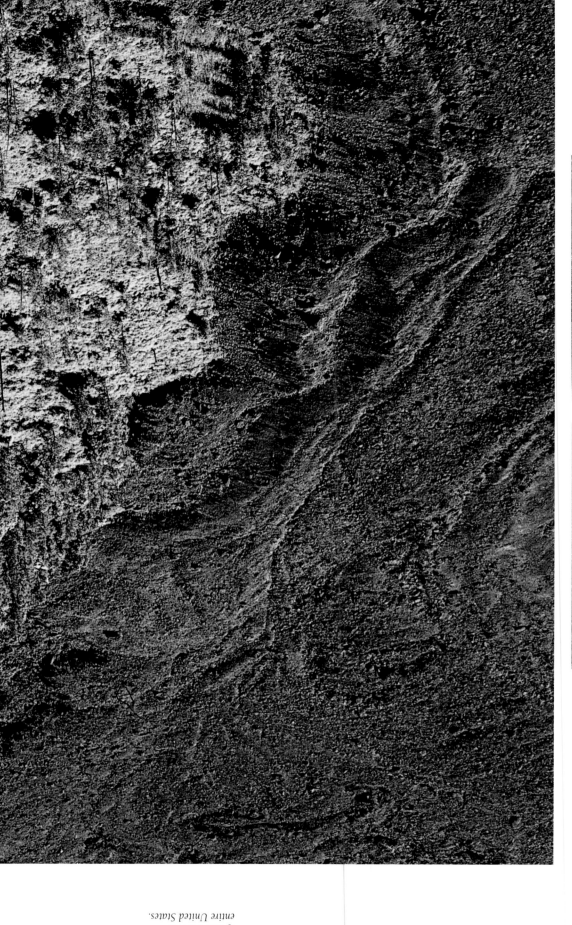

28 top A mute witness to the islands beauty dominates a panoramic view in the Hawaii Volcanoes National Park, which covers 234 square miles.

28 center The surface of lava flows on Kilauea solidify upon contact with the air, hiding the activities of the still partially fluid underlying lava.

28 bottom The Hawaii Volcanoes National Park was established in 1916, and protects many rare species. In all, the relatively small archipelago has more endangered species than the entire United States.

28-29 A kipuka bristling with medium-height trees has been spared by the lava flows that completely surround it.

BIG ISLAND

30-31 The lava in
the caldron of Puu
O'o constantly boils
and bubbles,
sometimes running
all the way down to
the coast, visible
from miles away.

31 top Pressurized
vapor clouds hover
around Kauleā's
caldera. Given the
unstable nature,
visits to the park
require caution.

31 center, top and
bottom Hawaii's
volcanoes famous
for being "good,"
but the calm can be
deceptive, as the
1790 and 1924
eruptions
demonstrated.

31 bottom Active
vents and solidifying
blocks of lava
spread about in a
tumbled setting of
stratified micro-
eruptions.

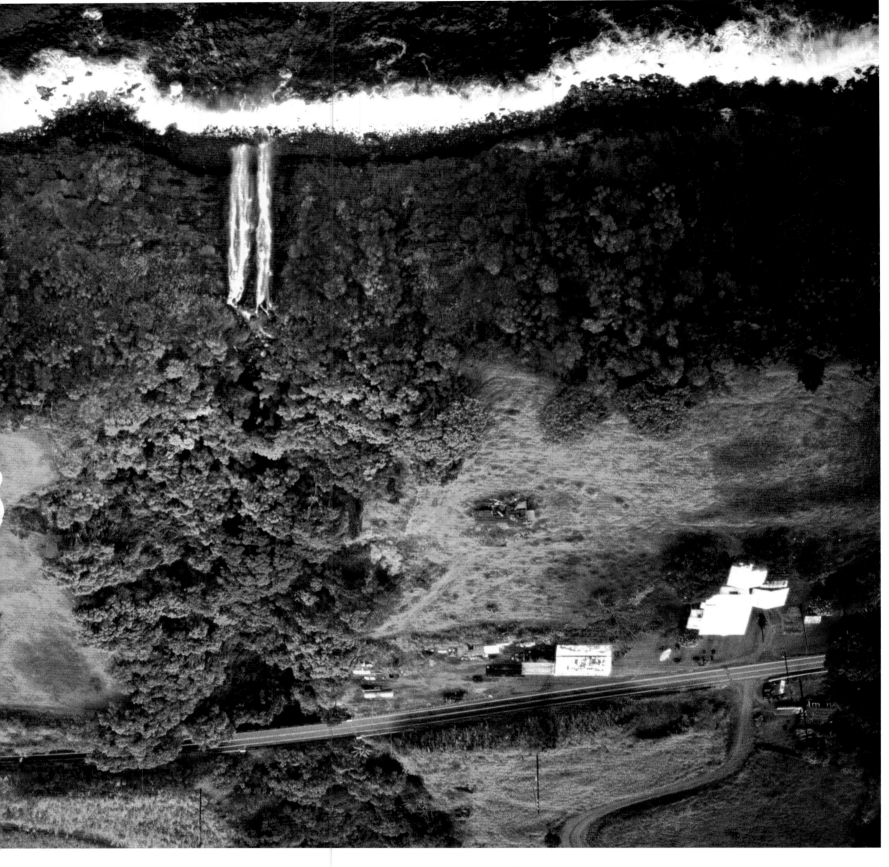

Seemingly undaunted by the nearby eruptive activities is Hilo, the gateway to Hawaii Volcanoes National Park, where the abundant rain has fostered the lush green Hilo Bay and gorgeous gardens of hibiscus. The town suffered devastating losses in 1946 and again in 1960, not from volcanoes, but from giant tsunamis, huge tidal waves of seismic origin. The downtown was completely destroyed, and when it was rebuilt, a large park and roadway were situated between the buildings and the shoreline to absorb future waves, some of which have reached up to 15 feet in height. North from Hilo, Akaka Falls State Park offers two waterfalls, one of which falls a splashy 442 feet into Kolekole Stream. Queen Kaahumanu Highway runs from Hilo around the south border to Kailua-Kona. It joins with two other state routes to form a circle around the entire island, forming what is often called the "Hawaii Belt."

Not far from Volcanoes National Park is the lovely and unique olivine Papakolea, Green Sand Beach. While the sand on most of the world's beaches consists almost entirely of quartz crystals, the Hawaiian Islands beaches are composed of volcanic mineral sands, ranging in color from white to gold to salt and pepper to black to the unique olive green. Olivine is an iron-magnesium silicate similar to that recently discovered on Mars; it is common in basalt lava. The flows from Mauna Loa can contain abundant quantities of these crystals. The volcanic cone, Puu Mahana associated with the Southwest Rift Zone of Mauna Loa, has been worn away by ocean waves forming the bay along the coast and eroding the volcanic sands to expose the olivine crystals that now form the beach. The black sand such as that at Punalu'u Black Sand

Beach is formed by eroded lava. Punalu'u is where whaling ships used to stop for fresh water at the adjacent ponds. Green sea turtles (*Chelonia mydas*) also use this beach as a nesting ground. Hapuna Beach is another wonderful sandy beach, half a mile long and almost 200 feet wide during the summer months. Swimming conditions here are usually excellent. This beach has frequently been voted the best beach in the US for its crystal-clear water and beautiful scenery. Snorkeling is great at the beach's south end where the fish are varied and there is a coral reef.

Sea turtles, manta rays, dolphins and varied shoals of multihued fish are seen at the state marine-life preserve at Kealakekua Bay. This bay is the infamous site where Captian Cook was killed on his first visit to the island February 14, 1779. Cook's party had arrived on board the *Resolution* and the *Discovery* during his third exploratory voyage, while the native islanders were celebrating their annual Makahiki festival honoring and thanking Lono, the god of agriculture and farming. Having landed ashore with such opportune timing, the locals greeted Cook and his crew as though they were sent by the gods and lavished them with gifts and supplies. The two ships left but soon after they encountered a storm, broke a mast and were forced to return to the island. With their mortality revealed the natives felt deceived and became hostile. A small boat from the *Discovery* was stolen, and Cook tried to kidnap a Kona chief, planning to exchange him for the boat. The resulting scuffle cost Cook his life. There is a multitude of stories claiming to describe what happened to Cook's body, which was never seen again. One version is that Cook was granted the Hawaiian funerary rights owed to a great chief; a contrary version is that he was eaten by cannibals. Neither account has

32-33 Gushing down from the slopes of Mauna Kea, a stream falls into the sea north of Hilo.

33 top left One of the 15 or so gulches through which flow the periodic waterways that radiate out from Mauna Kea's north slope.

33 top right and bottom Facing onto the Hamakua Coast, Hilo is a lovely town famous for its gardens, whose luxuriant growth is favored by the decidedly humid climate.

ever been confirmed. A tall white obelisk marks the rocky coastal site on which he fell. One point of interest is that in Hawaiian, Captain Cook is called Lono, a major god in Tahitian religious beliefs, and he was received as such at Hiki-au *heiau* (temple) where the ritual of human sacrifice was carried out: this temple is now a state monument.

The Waimea area of the north coast of Hawaii is cowboy country, and the only characteristic that differentiates the *panio-los* (Hawaiian cowboys) from their American Midwest counterparts is the feathered lei the island cowboys wear around their cowboy hats. Captain George Vancouver is responsible for introducing long-horned cattle to Hawaii in 1793. By 1809 the cows had become feral and King Kamehameha (born c. 1750, died 1819, known as Kamehameha the Great) hired a 19-year-old New England sailor named John Parker to round them up. Young Parker did more than round up the king's cattle; he went on to marry the king's granddaughter. Eventually 225,000 acres were to become the Parker Ranch, the largest and most famous ranch on the island, complete with some 50,000 head of cattle, 850 miles of fence, several hundred working horses and a couple dozen full-time cowboys. The ranch produces about 10 million pounds of beef a year.

In addition to beef, Hawaii is widely recognized for other products. The Kona Coast (on the island's west) produces macadamia nuts in its northern part and world-famous Kona coffee in its southern part. Besides these and other products, Hawaii's western coast has also produced notable warriors, including Kamehameha the Great, born at Kohala.

*34 and 35
Whimsical designs
created by the
archipelago's
complex geological
activity characterize
the countryside of
Big Island, full of
rare animal and
plant species.*

*36-37 Uncultivated
areas stand out
among the green of
the farms. Observed
from the sky, where
nature has not been
the author of
natural "pictures,"
the hand of man has
intervened.*

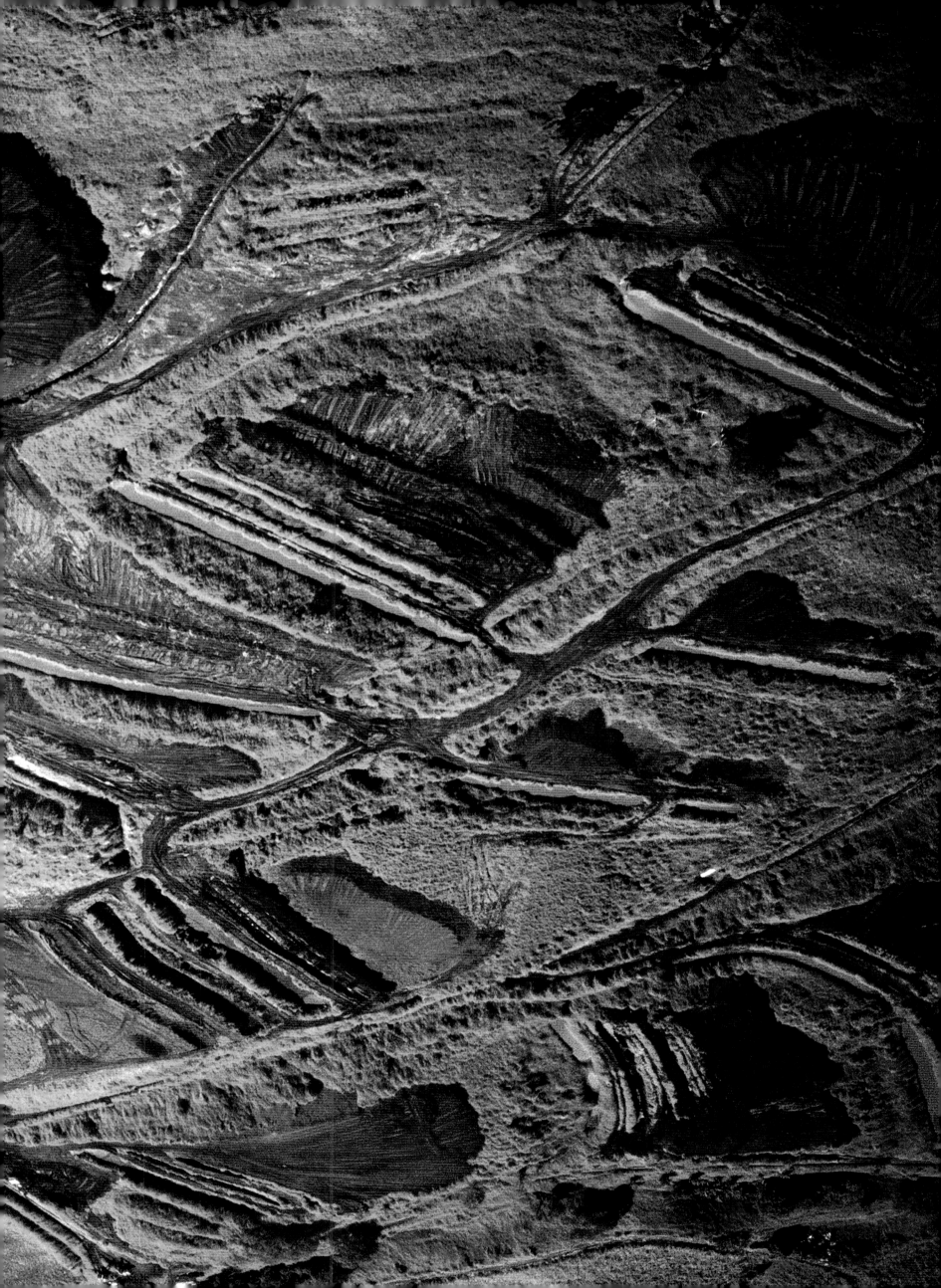

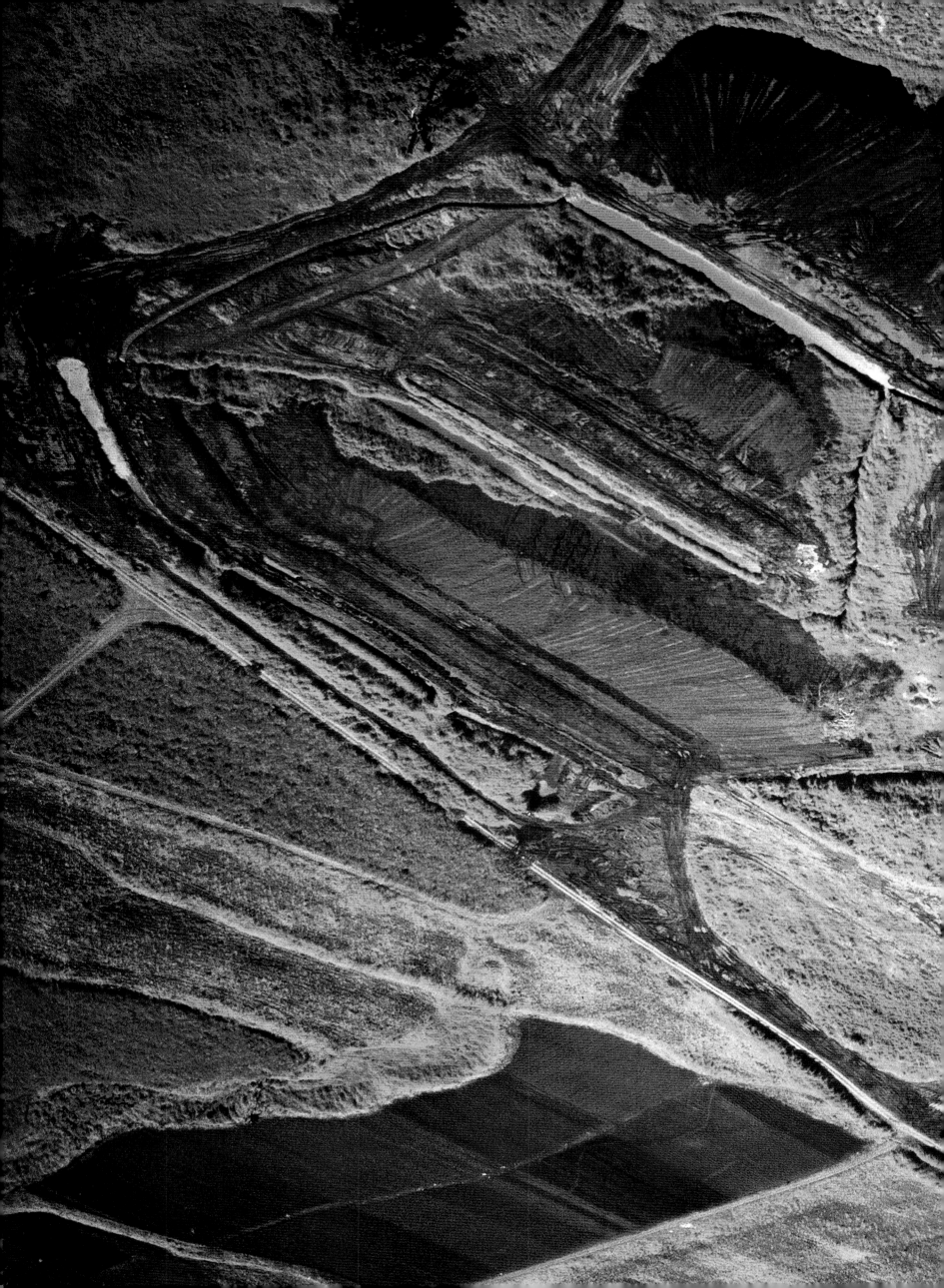

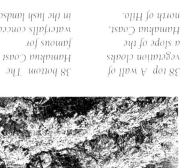

38 top A wall of
vegetation cloaks
a slope of the
Hamakua Coast,
north of Hilo.

38 bottom The
Hamakua Coast is
famous for
waterfalls concealed
in the lush landscape.

38-39 Akaka Falls
Park boasts sheer
waterfalls
enhancing one of
the Hawaiian
Islands' most
luxuriant
environments.

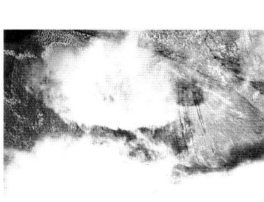

42-43 Cultivated lots line the seashore in Honoka'a, continuing toward the northwest end of Big Island. This orderly countryside covers an area that experiences the Hamakua Coast's humid climate. Honoka'a lies in the lee of the dormant Mauna Kea, which looms to the south.

40-41 The spectacular Kohala Mountain range reaches its maximum height at 5499 feet, in the peak of Kauu O Kaleihooliole.

40 top and bottom Narrow little streams mark the cliffs of the Kohala Mountains, in the northwestern portion of Big Island.

BIG ISLAND

44-45 Resorts, condominiums, houses, and hotels dot the Kona Coast, on the downwind (west) side of Big Island.

45 top and bottom Today it's lively and features large shopping centers and hotels, but two centuries ago Kamahameha the Great valued

Kailua-Kona for its tranquility.

46-47 A sea of solid lava covers the area inland from Kamoamoa Beach.

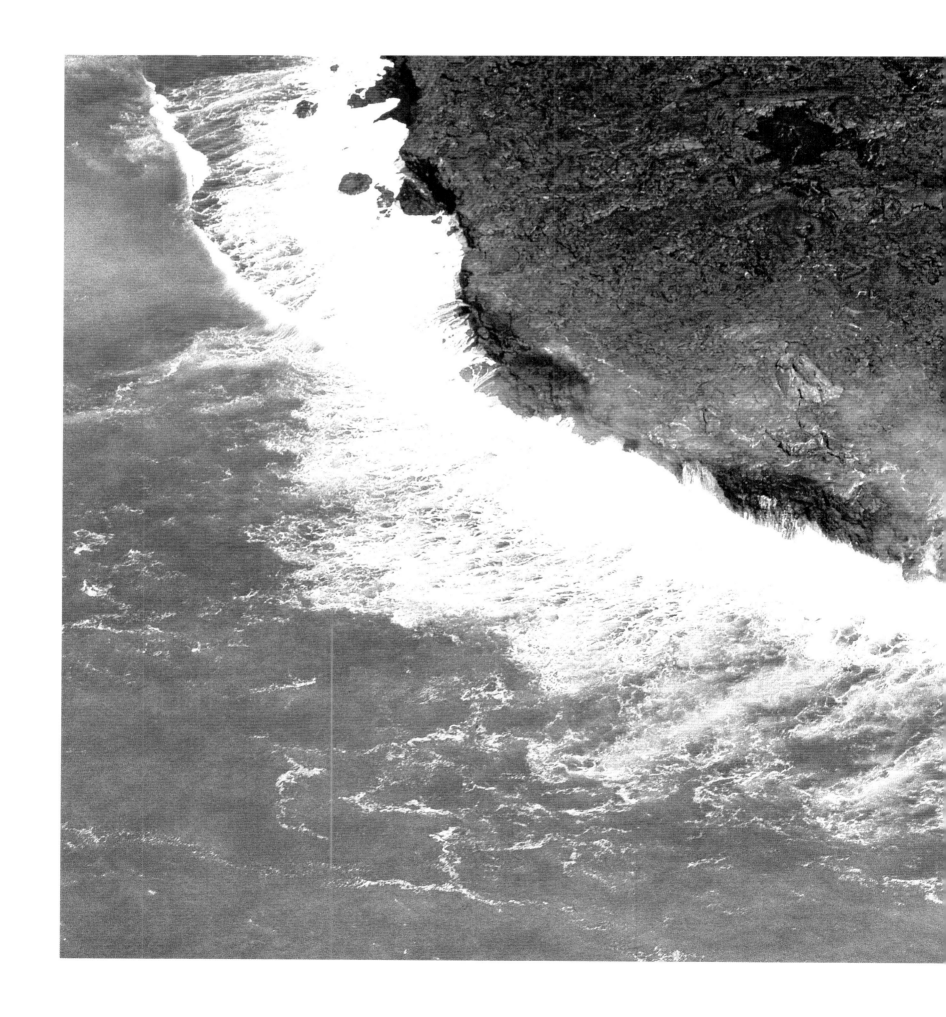

48-49 Big Island
often reveals itself
as the youngest of
the Hawaiian
Islands: Kamoamoa
Beach, for example,
continues to grow
wider.

49 The downwind
coast of Hawaii is
the driest part of the
otherwise humid
coastline that
stretches to the east.
The volcanoes create
a barrier to the trade
winds that influence
the climate.

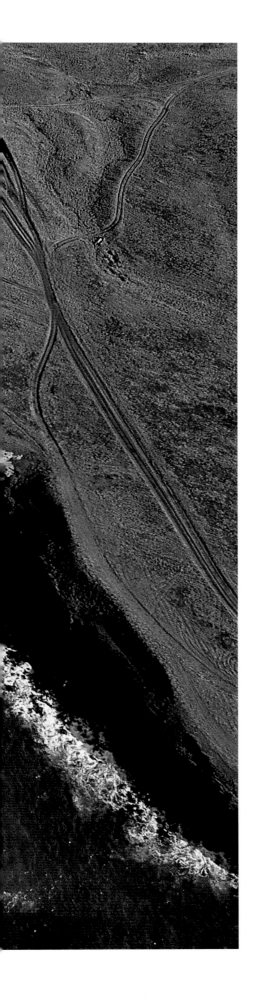

50-51 Papakolea, or Green Beach, was created out of fire and sea. The ocean waves have created the bay and eroded the volcanic sands, bringing out olive-green colored crystals.

51 Green is an understatement in describing Papakolea: the colors of the crystals that tint the sand are widely varied, including white, gold, black, and sulfur yellow.

52-53 On the Hamakua Coast, Wapio Bay opens at the mouth of the narrow valley of the same name, the biggest and only relatively accessible one among the seven magnificent valleys in the area.

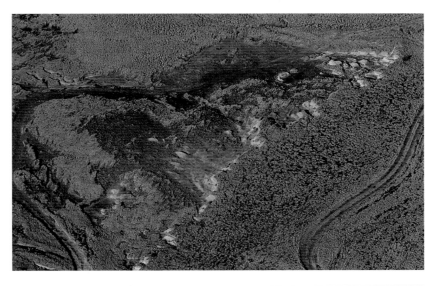

Maui has a special relationship with the sun, which seems to shine on this island with a special warmth. When the demigod Maui lassooed the sun and forced it to slow its journey across the Hawaiian sky, long summer days were bestowed upon the island. Legend has the island's highest point to be where the sun resides. This point is the summit of the Haleakala Crater, whose name in Hawaiian means the 'House of the Sun.'

The largely unexplored mountains of West Maui boast peaks that were once regarded

of the Kings, where ceremonial burials of royalty took place.

Iao Needle, a sharply pointed 1,200-foot high mount, provided a natural altar that was once ablaze with bamboo torches and wrapped in the echoing chants of prayer during the ceremonies.

The Iao Stream is the largest of the four major streams that streak down the West Maui Mountains to arrive at the ocean forming the Na Wai Eha (Four Waters) valleys of Maui: they are the Iao, Waikapu, Waiehu and Waihe'e valleys. Maui, one of the youngest of the Hawaiian Islands, was formed by two shield volca-

as the juncture between Heaven and Earth.

The highest peak is Pu'u Kukui 'the Hill of Light.' And the most powerful Hawaiian god was referred to as The Supreme Light, or Iao.

The valley that now carries this divine name is the Valley

noes that as they simultaneously grew higher and higher above sea level with each eruption they also grew closer and closer together. Finally they became joined at their isthmus, creating a large valley that characterizes Maui as 'the Valley of the Isles.'

Haleakala Crater, at the summit of the East Maui Volcano, is the highest point on the island at 10,023 feet above sea level, almost twice the height of the highest non-volcanic peak on the island.

East Maui Volcano has an area of 570 sq. miles, encompassing 77 percent of the island's surface area. Its volume is 7,200 cubic miles of which 97 percent is below sea level. It is the largest dormant volcano crater in the world and its awakening

Within this wilderness are some of the island's hardiest native flora and fauna. They have found a niche in the harsh environment of the high-alpine, or Aeolian zone, a dry, barren area that offers strata upon which only a few plant species such as the native ahinahina or silversword (*Argyroxiphium sandwichense macrocephalum*) can establish themselves. This fuzzy silver plant may take up to 50 years to mature, at which time it blossoms with hundreds of

It is in this type of shrub cover that is the ideal habitat for the Nene (*Branta sandwichensis*), the endangered Hawaiian goose. This land bird has adapted to the harsh lava terrain by evolving to have somewhat clawed feet and modifying its wings for shorter flights. It has been brought back from the brink of extinction through a restoration program that has protected the species from hunters since 1949.

is the subject of active debate. It is thought to have last erupted in 1790. Haleakala National Park was established in 1961 after formerly being within the boundaries of Hawaii National Park. Haleakala was given its own designation as a national park and in 1980 was designated an International Biosphere Reserve. It encompasses 30,183 acres, of which 24,719 are considered wilderness.

pink- to wine-red-colored flowerheads—and then the entire plant dies. The reproduction of the plant relies upon its seeds, and in any given year the population of silversword varies from zero to thousands of specimens. Descending into the sub-alpine microenvironment the scene becomes greener with a proliferation of shrubs and grasses that are found nowhere else on earth.

56 Windsurfers ride the ocean off Maui. The island boasts more than 80 beaches suitable for swimming and water sports, the largest number in any Hawaiian island.

56-57 Like the wings of strange water butterflies, the windsurfers' sails catch the breeze as they skim across the waves off Maui. The immense hump of Haleakala is silhouetted in the background.

58-59 Twin ponds stand on a crest in the Iao Valley. The mountain chain takes its name from the god of light, a supreme divinity in the Hawaiian pantheon.

60-61 Ripples of volcanic rock (traditionally and still compared to rays of light) climb toward the highest point in the area: Puu Kukui, the "Hill of Light," 5788 feet high.

62

62-63 Haleakala is
the biggest extinct
volcano in the
world. The surface
area of the shell at
the summit is so
vast that it seems
like an alien desert
planet.

63 top The
Haleakala
Observatory, at
10,000 feet high, is
surrounded by crisp
air that is about
only one fifth as
dense as the
troposphere, the
primary cloud-
forming zone.

63 bottom
Repulsive and yet
fascinating,
Haleakala did not
fail to attract the
Hawaiians, who
saw divine
dwellings and
wonderful natural
temples in its peaks.

The two sides of Haleakala are in direct contrast to each other. The dry forest zone on the leeward slopes of Haleakala receives only 20 to 60 inches of annual rainfall.

Kaupo Gap is one of the last remnants of the true dry-forest ecotype; most of this forest type has been lost to invasive, non-native plants, grazing animals, and fire. The windward slopes are covered by rainforest that receives an annual rainfall of 120 to 400 inches per year. The Ohi'a tree (*Metrosideros polymorpha*), possibly the most common Hawaiian native plant, derives its botanical name *polymorpha* from the wide variations of color and form it plant assumes. The bottle-brush flowerheads range in color from stunning crimson red to sunny yellow to delicate white, while the even more diverse leaves can be red or green, fuzzy or smooth and round or pointed. They dominate the canopy on Haleakala, grading downward to mingle with koa trees. On a note of interest, the koa tree is botanically different from one island to another. In the 1920s a reforestation project collected koa seeds from around the islands to replant in various locations. This mixed the species and now botanists are confronted with the chalenge of determining whether a particular koa stand is native to its home island or is

actually from the koa of another island. One of the most intact rain forest ecosystems in Hawaii is the Kipahulu Valley, where numerous species of rare birds and insects find refuge. Waterfalls and streams connect a chain of freshwater pools surrounded by rolling grasslands and lush forests. Ginger and ti grow wild in the forests of kukui, mango, guava and bamboo. Beach naupaka, false kamani and pandanus cling to the rugged coastal cliffs.

Another gorgeous site is Hana Valley, with its luscious green forests bordering a red-sand beach along the teal-green bay. The garnet-red sands at the base of Kauiki are the eroded sediment of the volcano and are symbolic of the bloodshed caused by the many wars waged between chiefs from Hana and other islands on and around Kauiki Head. The wife of Kamehameha the Great was born in a cave at Kauiki Head in 1772 during a period of war. She would eventually cause the collapse of the ancient religious law (*kapu*) through the single act of dining with her stepson; it was strictly forbidden for the sexes to dine together and when this meal was not followed by divine retribution, the people rioted and destroyed their temples. The Hana Forest Reserve aims to protect native forest species; unfortunately most of the plants seen growing around Hana and along the Hana Highway from Hana north to Huelo are paperbark and eucalyptus and, at historic Kauiki Head, ironwood trees, which are all native to Australia. South of Hana at Kipahulu, the dominant tree is the South American kiawe (*Prosopis pallida*) also known as algarroba or mesquite. Not far from Hana is Kipahulu, a dense largely unexplored rainforest. One of the most spectacular sites in the forest is the 400-foot Waimoku Falls. Several pools are linked like a string of pearls spilling into each other until the last one gracefully flows into the ocean.

On the other side of the is-

land is Kapalua, a 23,000-acre working pineapple plantation.

In 1992, the Maui Land & Pineapple Company dedicated 8,661 acres of native forest to the Nature Conservancy of Hawaii, creating Pu'u Kukui Nature Preserve. This protected area is home to several rare native species of plants and animals, including several native bird species, rare terrestrial snails, and many native plants, 18 of which are limited to West Maui and one is the very last in the world of its species—*Lobelia gloria montis*. There is also an abundance of ferns; one in six Hawaiian native plants is a fern! The tenacious *Achyranthes splendens* grows on the dry side of Pu'u Kukui, out of the dry lava boulders and rubble where it seems incredible that any plant could grow. The Maui parrotbill (*Pseudonestor xanthophrys*) is now found only here, in a single flock of about 500 birds. The Ponu La'au alani or Alani longhorned beetle (*Plagithmysus alani*) is preyed upon by a species of parrotbill, and now the beetle too is endangered. Mauna Kahalawai rises right in-

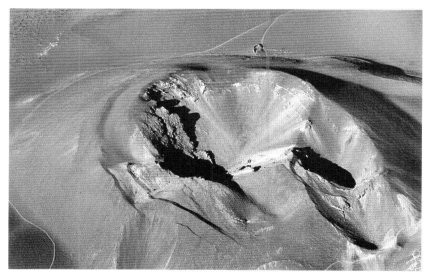

to the trade winds that at the summit can blow at up to 50 miles per hour; the peak receives up to 600 inches of rain per year (the annual average is 350 inches). The wet bogs of Pu'u Kukui are treasure troves of biological diversity. Every foot of accumulated organic material represents 10,000 years of growth. No one may walk across the bog; visitors must stay on the two-mile long boardwalk but from the sky the view is open and free and off the summit of Pu'u Kukui, Lanai and Molokai can be seen across the channel.

64 left top and bottom Small craters spread around the summit attest to the past activity of "young" Haleakala, born from the seabed one million years ago.

64 right The lowest temperature in the Hawaiian Islands, 12°F, has been recorded at the extensive remains of the volcano, whose name means "House of the Sun."

64-65 Haleakala Crater Road winds up around tight curves toward the upper area of the volcano. Beyond its border, the crater stretches as far as the horizon, an out-of-this-world place.

66 Wild Kahakuloa Bay is almost completely free of human settlement. Only a winding road links the zone to the rest of the island.

66-67 Kahakuloa Promontory extends out to the north of the West Maui Mountains. In some points, the territory is so impenetrable that it has yet to be explored.

Nearby Lahaina was Hawaii's capital prior to 1845 and was the first port that American whalers came to. The *Balena*, from Massachusetts, was the first that touched in, way back in 1818. Whaling soon became one of the dominant activities off the Maui coast, and must have been a horrific experience for the natives.

Despite their excellent fishing skills, they respected whales and never hunted them; if one were to ever wash ashore it was deemed the property of the king. Thanks to the Endangered Species Act and the 1973 ban on whaling, the populations of these still endangered species have stabilized. The humpback whale (*Megaptera novaeangliae*) is the third most endangered whale in the world, with an international population of only 7,000 to 8,000. These whales can be seen off Maui's shores during their winter migration from Alaska, breaching their 100,000-pound, 60-foot long bodies out of the waters, creating fantastic crashing scenes and waving their flukes to the delight of fortunate whale watchers. Many other whales are found in the waters of the Hawaiian archipelago, including the false killer whale (*Pseudorca crassidens*), the melon-headed whale (*Peponocephala electra*), and the sperm whale (*Physeter marocephalus*).

At the peak of its whaling era, Lahaina had an atmosphere of exploitation and debauchery. The Yankee Pacific whaling fleet took up its principal anchorage here between the 1820s and the 1860s, with the peak year being 1846 when 429 whalers called in at the harbor. The thousands of sailors who caroused the streets in search of hard liquor and women proclaimed that there was "no God west of the Horn" and conducted themselves accordingly. Eventually the missionaries stepped in and cleaned up the town, but not without violent resistance from the seamen. The ensuing riots are legendary. Today Lahaina still has the flavor of an old fishing town, but today instead of whaling ships pleasure boats are anchored offshore. Snorkeling, diving, whale watching, and the nearby Kaanapali and Wailea resort areas and golf courses have replaced the previous century's notorious pastimes. Kaanapali was once the holiday resort of Hawaiian royalty. Here they surfed the impressively high rolling waves and held luaus and pig roasts along the immaculate three-mile-long beach. They would also race their long outrigger canoes in the channel between Maui and Lanai.

68-69 The impetuous waves of the upwind Maui coast have ceaselessly been sculpting a promontory out of the Keanae Peninsula.

69 top A volcanic cone marked by lumps of lava dominates Makena Beach from the north, at the western base of Haleakala.

69 center From McGregor Point, panoramic view ranges extend across the open ocean: this is an excellent spot for observing whale migrations.

69 bottom The lovely loop of Molokini, a caved-in volcano cone, is like a natural aquarium full of life and is, luckily, protected by law.

70 The Kapalua
Coast, West Maui's
westernmost point,
features five
magnificent
crescent-shaped
bays. The area was
the world's first
certified protected
environment—and
sets an urgent
example to many
other endangered
natural areas.

70-71 Lush and
softly rippled, the
Keanae Peninsula
extends out into the
ocean from the base
of Haleakala's
northern slopes,
barely visible in the
background under a
hood of low clouds.

72 Large hotels have sprung up around Kama'ole, in the Kihei areai. This spot on South Maui's north coast of is renowned for easy access to three beach parks.

72-73 Built to offer every possible recreational activity, Kama'ole is a center for beaches suitable for several kinds of water sports.

74 Yachts, motorboats, and a museum-quality brig tied up along the shore of Lahaina. During the 1800s, at the height of the old Hawaiian kingdom, Lahaina flourished as a whaling port.

75 Resorts stand in zones with calm waters, where everyone can take a swim. On the other hand, some beaches on Maui can be dangerous during certain times of the years because of the waves.

76-77 A mosaic of colors heralds the Maui coast to those who arrive from the bay of Maalea. The flat area of the island extends before them, contained between the two volcanoes that created it.

On the surface, Lanai is the place for the rich and famous, but behind the island's glamorous façade lurk ghosts, demons and Lanai was once thought to be uninhabitable; prior to the 1500s Hawaiians considered this island to be the domain of demons and evil spirits. The first resident of Lanai was the rebellious son of a Maui king. He was banished to this demon-ridden island as punishment for his unacceptable and disobedient behavior. Through acts of courage and ritual, the boy was able to cleanse the island and eventually made it habitable. Soon, it was even fought over; the Big Island Chief Kalaniopuu raided Lanai, killing almost all who lived there in the process.

The future Hawaiian king, Kamehameha, was one of the chief's warriors, and he too would return in later years to conquer the island during his unification campaign. This island would become King Kamehameha's favorite fishing location.

There are remnants of the ancient fishing villages that once sustained the early economy, but it was the pineapple industry that really took hold of the little island of Lanai. After the Dole Company, founded by James Dole (1857-1958)), began operations in 1922, Lanai became known as the archipelago's pineapple bas-

work on the plantations.

Palawi Basin, the broad fertile basin where the pineapples grew so abundantly, is in the caldera of the ancient Palawai volcano. This single volcano formed Lanai about 1.5 million years ago, giving this island a rather distinctive and unusual formation and configuration compared to the archipelago's other islands. The summit of Lanaihale ("House of Lanai") is at 3,370 feet, and from this vantage much of Lanai is visible on a clear day, along with five other islands.

Maunalei Gulch is a distinctive landmark; it was here that the island's defenders were un-

ket, and for the next 65 years it produced an average of 25 million pineapples per year. Today no commercial pineapple operation exists on Lanai and all that remains are the empty, misty fields and the ghost towns of homes that once housed the families of the thousand or so workers Dole brought to the island to

able to stop the advance of Kamehameha the Great's warriors in his quest to unite the Hawaiian Islands in the late 18th and early 19th centuries. Legends and stories haunt some of the impressively high cliffs (the tallest sea cliff is Plai Kaholo, at 1,000 feet) that give a rugged chiseled quality to this island.

The towering sea stack called Puu Pehe (Sweetheart Rock) gets its name from the legend of the beautiful Maui girl who was stolen away by a young Lanai warrior. He hid her up on the cliff — only to lose her to the sea in a storm whose waves swept her to her death. Heartbroken, the warrior threw himself from the cliff and some believe that his spirit still searches the waves for his love. Kahekili's Jump is a 62-foot cliff named after a mighty Maui chief who would leap off cliffs as a show of bravado. Ancient warriors would test their courage by jumping from this particular cliff. Not only did the cliff's height above sea level demand courage, but also the need to clear the vicious ledge

below the top; it was an obstruction that would kill a timid jumper.

Other spectral presences of old Lanai might be found still lurking about Keomuku ghost town. In the late 1890s, when the Maunalei Sugar Company built and ran a C-class sugar plantation, Keomoku was a leading city in Lanai. The population

of the then small community of fishermen and farmers increased from about 174 to 2000. The mill was successful until about 1901, when construction of a railroad along the coast began. The company damaged or disturbed the sacred stones of a *heiau* (temple).

The Hawaiians believed that the gods were angered by this

disrespect: the mill's drinking water immediately and mysteriously turned salty and the population was devastated by illness. Maunalei Sugar shut down in 1901. Little remains today except the carefully restored small wooden Malamalama church tucked away under the coconut fronds.

The island's developed area is near the center. There Lanai city, the island's only city, is growing to meet the increasing demands spurred by tourism, five-star hotels, and two championship golf courses. Much of the employment that is available to Lanai's native population is in the service industry catering to tourists.

Lanai was for a long time quite undeveloped and elegantly rustic. The ruggedness of the

coastline, skirted with impassible cliffs, prevented any road from circumnavigating the island, and thus its natural beauty and landscapes are less encroached upon than in many of the larger islands. The lama (persimmon) and olupua (olive) are native varieties that still survive thanks to the foresight of the pioneer ranch manager and naturalist George C. Munro. He protected the plants by building fences around them to prevent them from being grazed upon by the wild deer and mouflon in the area. From 1911 through 1935 George Munro fenced large sections of what in 1991 became Kanepu'u Forest Preserve, which contains the largest remnants of the olopua/lama (*Nestegis/Diospyros*) dryland forest that

80-81 Bustling and sophisticated, Lanai City provides a cheerful contrast with areas not yet recovered from the demise of the pineapple industry.

81 top Lanai's rather low-lying interior features a fantastic open countryside. Lacking a coastal road, the island has remained largely wild.

81 bottom A vehicle spraying pesticides works through cultivated farmland. Local agriculture is slowly moving toward a comeback.

once covered large portions of the lowlands of Lanai as well as Maui, Molokai and Kahoʻolawe. The preserve is home to 49 plant species found only here, including four endangered plants: the fragrantly flowered naʻu, Hawaiian gardenia, (*Gardeniabrighamii*); iliahi or sandalwood (*Santalum freycinetianum* var. *Lanaiense*); the vining *Bonamia menziesii* and the maʻo hau hele (*Hibiscus brackenridgei* ssp. *brackenridgei*). Though not native to the islands, the presence of the characteristic Norfolk and Cook Islands pines of Lanai is also owed to Munro's green thumb. Two native birds are seen at Kanepuʻu: the pueo or short-eared owl (*Asio flammeus sandwichensis*), and the kolea or Pacific golden-plover (*Pluvialis fulva*).

Lanai's 47 miles of coastline should not go unnoticed. Hulopoe Beach is among the island's most popular, and the state marine conservation district works there to protect the valuable marine habitat. As a result, there is fabulous snorkeling charmed by frequent sitings of spinner dolphins (*Stenella longirostris*). Shipwreck Beach is also famous, easily recognizable by the World War II Liberty ship rusting offshore where it was stranded so many years ago. The first wrecks occurred here in the 1820s, when British and American ships struck the reef. This eight-mile stretch of the shore is a haven for beach-combers; they will find everything from nautilus shells to timbers and assorted ocean-going debris.

At the Kuanalu National Historic Landmark, a shrine honoring fishing marks the site of an ancient fishing village. This landmark is famous for having some of ancient Hawaii's most impressive and best-preserved archeological ruins and warrior-featuring petroglyphs. About 86 house foundations and 35 stone shelters are found on both sides of

Kaunolu Gulch. The site also consists of a lookout tower, detached pens and garden patches, trail remnants, gravesites, burial caves and the remains of Halulu *heiau* (temple), named after a mythical man-eating bird. The royal retreat King Kamehameha the Great is thought to have stood on the eastern edge of Kaunolu Gulch, overlooking the rocky shore facing Kahekili's Leap. Not far from here are the abandoned fishing villages of Lopa, Naha and Keomuku, all of which are presumed to be guarded by the *mana*, the spiritual power, of their former residents. There is a rumor in these parts that if people climb the coconut trees here without first reciting the proper prayers, they will never climb back down.

Lanai's mystery is further heightened by peculiar formations and patterns of large, irregularly shaped volcanic boulders mysteriously strewn about the crusted lava terrain of a remote canyon area called Keahi Kawelo, "the Garden of the Gods." It is named in keeping with an ancient legend that claims the rocks and boulders were dropped from the sky by the gods tending their gardens. The site was once revered as sacred, and the cause of the bizarre formations was long a mystery. However, scientists have explained how strong volcanic eruptive forces followed by thousands of years of erosion created the strange landscape of pinnacles and buttes of dazzling colors—brilliant red, orange, ocher, purple and yellow—that are seen today.

A popular diving spot that teems with bright tropical fish (and frequently with sharks) is Little Shark Island. Its dorsal fin can just be seen off Lanai's leeward coast; however, this little island is less recognizable than the more distinctively shark-shaped island of Molokai.

82-83 A rusting World War II freighter sits on Shipwreck Beach, a known hazard for shipping.

83 Long ribs of lava emerge along Shipwreck Beach, facing the treacherous Kalohi Channel, which separates Lanai from Molokai.

*84 top and bottom
The deserted
beaches of Lanai
offer miles of open
space, interrupted
by the intriguing
remains of the
abandoned villages
of fishermen.*

*85 Gentle surf
laps Lanai's ochre-
colored beaches,
which alternate
with rocky inlets
and cliffs along the
island's 47-mile
perimeter.*

een from the air, Molokai has the easily identifiable shape of a shark, with its head facing east, its tail in the west, and a dorsal fin rising from its back on the wet north shore. Throughout its history, this island has remained quite underpopulated, not because its shark-like shape hinted at any danger in the waters, but rather from fear of the *kahuna* (priests), who at one time practiced a wicked type of sorcery on Molokai. The largest temple on the island, Iliiliopai, whose altars "ran red with human blood," was notorious throughout the islands. The most powerful of the *kahuna*, Lanikaula,

is buried here under a grove of sacred kukui trees.

However, Molokai was geographically strategic and a desirable acquisition for the ancient Hawaiian chiefs. Eventually Kamehameha the Great arrived in 1795 and claimed Molokai as part of his kingdom. The island's economy was a subsistence one based on taro farming and fishing. Ancient fishponds can be found all along the eastern coastline. They are being examined today for their ecological approach to fish farming. When Del Monte established its great pineapple plantations, Molokai's economy changed, but after the plantation shut down in 1982, the island was left largely undeveloped and

of thundering, tumbling water. All this splendor is found in an area a mere 38 mile by 10 miles, much of which is still remarkably wild.

Owing to its rockiness, Molokai is graced with dramatic valleys best seen from the sky as few have road access. One of the most spectacular and renowned is

Wailau. The 4,970-foot cliff walls that enclose this valley make it inaccessible except by boat or helicopter or by a very strenuous hike. The green and black cliff walls enshrining the long curve of the black sand beach are brilliantly lit by an unrivaled array of intermingling sunbeams, tropical showers, and rainbows.

economically depressed. But the few residents appreciate the simple and ecologically sustainable way of life that Molokai offers and don't seem to be seeking any great changes.

Molokai's pristine quality makes it the most precious charm on the bracelet of the Hawaiian archipelago; in many places its natural beauty is as vibrant and unspoiled as it was when the first Hawaiians arrived. The island's intrinsic magnificence is seen in its boastfully tall sea cliffs, some of the highest in the world, from which leap bold *wailele* or waterfalls. The Hawaiian word *wailele* means "leaping waters," a most appropriate description as the trade winds tease and toy with the cascading waters, engaging them in an aerial aquatic dance. The longest waterfall in Hawaii is Kahiwa, "the Sacred One," a 1,750 feet flume

86 top and bottom From the air, Molokai looks like a natural fortress, protected by coastal bastions that abruptly rise up for hundreds of feet.

86-87 The coast of Kalaupapa is typical of Molokai, impenetrable and wild. At its highest point, the cliffs rise 2953 feet.

88-89 Wide crescent-shaped bays embrace the Kalaupapa coast, as magnificent as its history is dramatic. In the past Hawaiians feared Molokai because the dreaded kahuna priests performed human sacrifices there.

90-91 *Large rugged plateau-like areas of Molokai are scarred by remote, deep valleys: practically untouched by man: this environment is home to plant species unique to Molokai.*

91 top *At times, the lush appearance of the Molokai's cliffs alternate with tracts of barren and uninviting coast, as in the area of Halawa, on the island's easternmost part.*

91 bottom *The rugged and varied topography of Molokai's eastern region (the most mountainous) results in part from abundant rain.*

Lying within the valley's lush greenery are ancient *heiaus* (temples) and remains of stonewall enclosures. The still intact *auwai* (irrigation canals) on parcels of land called *kuleana* were abandoned by the taro-farming people who once inhabited the valley, the last of whom left in the 1920s. The taro still grows wild, as does the banana, guava, rose apple, mountain apple, papaya and avocado.

Wailau Volcano, or East Molokai Volcano, is overlapped by Lanai, Haleakala and Mauna Loa volcanoes and makes up the eastern two-thirds of this last cone. The summit of the now dormant Mauna Loa rises 4,970

feet above sea level. It is believed that a giant landslide removed much of the north flank of the Wailau Volcano. Evidence exists on the seafloor over a hundred miles off the coast of East Molokai, where there are landslide blocks that presumably collapsed off the north coast of East Molokai during this monster landslide and rolled on for miles at high speeds. These prehistoric landslides caused by the rains and the legendary northern swells are thought to have cut the cliffs that have shaped the fantas-

tic landscape of northern Molokai. Because it rains so much of the time, the lyrical sounding name given to Pelekunu Valley actually means "moldy smell." The valley is crampingly narrow, with walls so high that only four or five hours of sunshine reach the floor. Two contrasting waterfalls cut the V-shaped valley: on one side of the narrow cleft the water falls gusty and explosive, crashing against the worn rocks; on the other side the water calmly pours over the top and follows a straight, smooth descent. The falls unite and create a deep gorge in the back of the valley, filling the black rocky pools with clear, cool waters. The jagged cliff-faces with their many crevices, rise skyward like sentinels guarding the dark hidden ravine. Halawa Valley is another noteworthy valley; it is one of the first settlements made by the early Polynesians. They lived here for thousands of years and had built at least 18 temples. They subsisted on fishing and harvesting their great fields of taro. The valley was abandoned in the mid-1900s when two successive tsunamis (one a 45-foot giant), wiped out the crops and forced the people to leave.

92 *East Molokai's nearly vertical spurs appear impossible to climb, but the cliff-clinging paths actually can be hiked. If the challenge seems too tough, then a see-it-from-the-air tour is the perfect answer.*

93 *Molokai is famous for its waterfalls. Wailele ("The Waters that Fall") pours down over the rock-face like a bridal veil. Over the millennia, the water has dug out amazing amphitheaters and circular pools, thanks to the porosity of the volcanic rock.*

The range of spectacular cliffs on Molokai's northern coast also set the scene for an ugly incident this beautiful island's history. This unfortunate stain is the island's former leper colonies.

One was at Kalaupapa on the north shore, at the base of the Makanalua Peninsula, which forms a natural prison surrounded by deathly surf and rip-tides and backed by a 2,000- to 3,000-foot sheer palisade.

Another colony was at Kalawoa, also on the north shore but in a less protected location on the eastern side of the peninsula; because of this, most of the members were eventually moved to Kalaupapa. After Europeans arrived, thousands of Hawaiians died of diseases brought from abroad; these

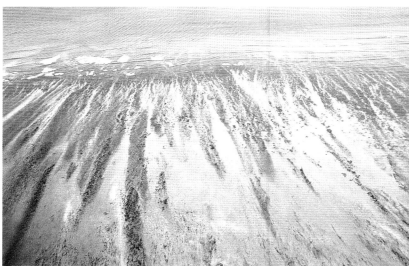

94 The calm, sparkling and calm waters that ripple over coastal shoals on Molokai can become raging walls of water: in 1946 and 1957, tsunami devastated the island's interior.

94-95 The thread-like arcs visible in the water are the low walls of fish pens, built according to an indigenous technique. The fish that manage to slip through the grates that close the openings of the "trap" grow larger over time and finally can no longer get out. This fish-farming technique dates back to the 15th century.

included leprosy (now known as Hansen's Disease), which caused such an epidemic that King Kamehameha V (1830-1872) had its unfortunate victims exiled. From 1866 (when Kalaupapa was founded) people inflicted with the disease were quarantined on the remote peninsula with very few amenities and very little aid. It wasn't until 1873, when Belgian priest Father Damien (the Rev. Joseph Damien de Veuster) arrived, that the members of the colony received compassionate care. He stayed with the colony until he died of the disease in 1889. In 1969 the quarantine restrictions were lifted and the colony was freed from restrictions. However, many of the longtime residents chose not to leave and fewer than a hundred still live there to this day. Kalaupapa is now a National Historic Park but is only reachable by small plane unless the visitor is sturdy enough to endure the steep hike or long mule ride.

Managed by the Nature Conservancy of Hawaii, the 2,774-acre Kamakpou Preserve protects some of the invaluable forests on Molokai. The preserve encompasses ecosytems from low-valley to high-summit rainforests, cloud forests, and the precious montane bog, Pepeopai. The bog's unique botany is incredible, with native plants found nowhere else in the world. Most of the plants are Lilliputian in size such as the bonsai-esque ohi'a tree that stands a mere four inches tall with bold scarlet blossoms that are almost larger than the tree

itself. To counter the still high plant-extinction rate on Molokai, the conservancy tries to remove non-native competitor plant species. However, island residents do not totally support the eradication of feral animals because many of them subsist by hunting pigs. These are an ecological problem; they root up the vegetation allowing erosion and destruction of the watersheds. Also managed by the Nature Conservancy are the Moomomi Dunes, an area representative of native strand vegetation. The dunes cover a windswept, salt-sprayed area of 920 acres of desert-like golden dunes brushstroked with mattes of low-growing hardy silvery green or pale silver plants. Hawaiian monk seals (*Monachus schauinslandi*) sunbathe and green sea turtles (*Chelonia mydas*) nest on the beach. Today sanderlings and plovers scurry along the shoreline but at one time, according to archeological evidence at the dunes, there were birds of a slightly different feather here, such as a flightless ibis, a four-foot goose that laid eggs the size of coconuts, a long-legged owl, and a sea eagle.

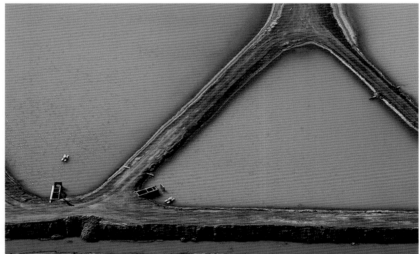

96-97 and 97 top Molokai's marshes are valuable biodiversity resources. The soft cloak of the vegetation broken by small pools hosting rare species is uniquely suited to creating needed microenvironments.

97 center and bottom In addition to Nature's impress, the face of Molokai has been marked by geometrical shapes created by aquaculture and new plantations, now thriving in the aftermath of the 1980s' agricultural crisis.

98-99 Deeply grooved by the forces of Nature, Molokai's volcanic spurs rise from lagoons teeming with life. Visible in the middle of the photo is a fish-pen barrier of madreporic rock.

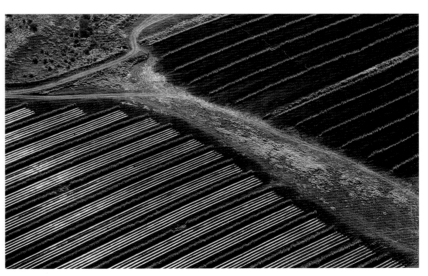

ahu's distinctive topography expresses the diversity of its personality. Wild, rugged mountain ranges and volcanic craters are in dramatic contrast to sophisticated modern cities marked by sleek steel skyscrapers, universities, and interstate freeways (that do not actually connect any two states!), and the island presents a complexion of natural exotic beauty, though not unmarked by the scars of war. Oahu's playful face is seen along its beaches full of surfers, vacationers, and in its many resorts. The island's quieter windward side is mostly green, freckled

world's most famous volcanic crater, and offers reputedly the world's best and most dangerous surfing; it is also the site of the only attack made on United States' territory in World War II —Pearl Harbor.

For some sixteen years after Captain Cook discovered Hawaii in 1778, the harbor of Honolulu remained unknown to the Europeans. Then Captain William Brown aboard the HMS *Jackal* discovered the quiet bay. Soon the little fishing village of Honolulu became the world's busiest whaling port and an entrepôt for guns, alcohol and other assorted destructive goods exchanged for

with farms and ranches.

Renowned for its scenic splendor, white-sand beaches and celebrated surf, Oahu is also the most settled of the Hawaiian Islands with 75 percent of the archipelago's population residing here along—with a significant number of endangered species such as the Hawaiian monk seal (*Monachus schauinslandi*). The island claims Diamond Head, the

commodities such as Hawaiian sandalwood, the heavy harvesting of which resulted in serious deforestation. Modern Honolulu prides itself on commerce: the city is considered the business and financial center of the Pacific. It is also the capital city of the State of Hawaii and has an international airport, a major port, and is the United States' Pacific Region military command center.

100 top Honolulu's downtown towers are silhouetted against a cobalt blue sky. This modern capital boasts one of the loveliest scenic and climatic locations in the world.

100 bottom Located between the Bay of Pearl Harbor and Honolulu, Oahu's international airport welcomes an average of 70,000 tourists a day to the capital of the islands.

100-101 "Waikiki" the name is among the exotic, magical few that lead everybody to dream: its charm derives from its extraordinary natural setting and its dynamic mix of cultures.

102-103 The contrast is breath-taking: beyond the summit of a line of sheer and ancient crests, the skyline of 20th century Honolulu is revealed. The mountain chain overlooking the city peaks in Konahuanui at 3104 feet.

104 Downtown Honolulu is a modern urban area, but perfectly "man-sized": its most apparent characteristic is availability of space—space generally used for relaxation.

104-105 and 105 top The Waikiki Beach skyscrapers, in some cases an attraction in themselves, border on a 2.5-mile uninterrupted expanse of sand: here the myth was born.

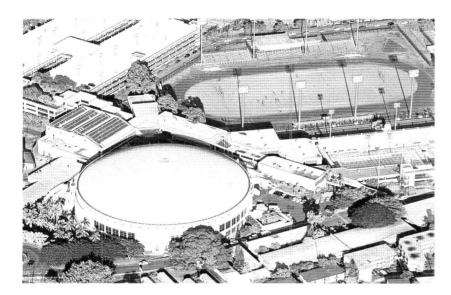

Abundant oyster beds gave the name *Wai Momi* or "pearl waters" to Pearl Harbor, the area now recognized for an act of lasting infamy. On December 7, 1941, Imperial Japanese forces devastated the American fleet killing 2,300 people, 68 of whom were civilians. The USS *Arizona* was bombed and sunk, taking with it 1,200 lives. Today the *Arizona* Memorial stands in tribute above the sunken ship in which the service men lie entombed. The 58,000-ton battleship, the USS *Missouri*, is berthed here to house a military museum. It is on the deck of this ship that General Douglas MacArthur received the unconditional surrender of Japan on September 2, 1945.

Long before these events, when the United States annexed Hawaii in 1898, the military established Pearl Harbor as a staging area for ships heading to Guam and the Philippines during the Spanish-American War.

106-107 The armored battleship USS Missouri remains a dignified memorial of December 7, 1941; the occasion of the horrific attack on Pearl Harbor.

107 top and bottom Today, Pearl Harbor continues to be an active military base,

but clearly it is also a memorial. The armored battleship USS Arizona, its superstructure hit, sank within a few minutes with 1,200 sailors aboard. The ship remains a unique underwater museum, in part for the number of lives commemorated.

108-109 *Hawaiian proportions: a broad valley opens toward the ocean on Oahu's mid-east coast, in the protected area of Kualoa State Park.*

109 top A red blanket of lava covers the Manauma Bay seabed, moved by a light current that maintains a sort of naturally created aquarium.

109 bottom The splendid Kahana valley enters into a universe of wild and challenging gorges and peaks, to be explored with care.

Kure Atoll, which is 1,367 miles away, is an almost completely circular shallow-water coral reef with several small islands rising from it. The atoll is closed to the public and most of the islands are designated as bird sanctuaries.

Oahu, like all the other Hawaiian Islands, was formed by volcanic activity of the Hawaiian hot spot, from where it has now shifted approximately 220 miles north owing to the continuous migration of the Pacific tectonic plate. In prehistoric times, half Oahu fell into the ocean, causing a massive tidal wave that washed over the island of Lanai. The sub-sequent landslides on Oahu created the jagged cliffs along much of the coastline. These dramatic contours prevent any road from completely circling the island's periphery. The Farrington Highway travels along the western coastline but at the westernmost tip it is interrupted by Kaena Point State Park, where the rugged terrain makes car travel difficult. However, from the air this natural area reserve offers scenic views of the topography and ancient temple ruins tucked away in the foliage.

The two distinctive mountain chains on Oahu are the Koolau and the Waianae ranges.

111 Since the end of the 1800s, the pineapple has represented an important source of income for the Hawaiian population, above all for Chinese and Japanese immigrants. After many plantations were abandoned at the end of the last century, Oahu, Maui, and Lanai remained the strongholds of this type of cultivation.

110 Besides its famous pineapples, inland Oahu features pleasant contrasts of color: the intense ochre of the soil and the plantations, the green of thriving plants, and the straw-yellow of ripening produce.

110-111 "Carpets" of plants are laid out in keeping with the conformation of the terrain on a pineapple plantation. Oahu's interior is largely dedicated to the cultivation of pineapples and sugar cane.

The Koolau Mountains run north to south almost the entire length of the island while the shorter range, belonging to the Waianae Range, are older and rounder and contain the island's tallest peak, Mount Kaala (4,025 feet). The range resulted from the upheaval of the ancient caldera, the center of which is now about five miles southwest of Mount Kaala, between the Lualualei and Waianae valleys. The original Waianae volcano formed over three million years ago. Because of its rounded conical shape, Mount Kaala resembles a volcano. The top of the mountain is hollowed out like a bowl and is tipping slightly toward the Waianae Valley. Within this bowl is a lush, humid, misty bog full of botanical treasures of native Hawaiian foliage. The Mount Kaala Natural Area Reserve is dedicated here to the conservation of this precious ecological system. The Laualualei Plateau in the interior of the island is in contrast with its exotic surroundings; its landscape has been extensively cultivated with an introduced plant species—the pineapple. It is believed that Polynesian settlers from Tahiti first brought the pineapple to Hawaii for cultivation, but it was James Dole (1857-1958) who made the fruit emblematic of Hawaii. He arrived in Oahu in 1898 and within three years had sown 12 acres in the Wahiawa Valley with 75,000 pineapples, producing 1,893 cans of the chunked fruit! Today both the Dole and Del Monte fruit companies exploit the area.

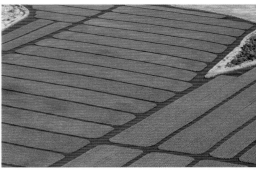

As well as mountain ranges, Oahu has several massive extinct volcanoes. The most noteworthy are Koko Head (642 feet), Punchbowl (500 feet) and Diamond Head (760 feet). While all three have their distinctions, Diamond Head is the most famous. The ancient Hawaiians gave the volcano the name *Lea'hi*, meaning "brow of the tuna," reflecting its shape. In the 1800s British sailors named it Diamond Head after mistaking the worthless calcite crystals they found there to be the much more valuable gemstone. This tuff cone (made from rock formed from compressed volcanic ash) became a dead volcano when it completely collapsed upon itself. This now dead crater is one of the most prominent features on Oahu's landscape. Punchbowl Crater is believed to have had a *heiau* (temple) at its summit where violators of the *kapu* (the sacred laws) were sacrificed and cremated. Ironically, today Punchbowl's summit is the site of the National Memorial Cemetery of the Pacific. It contains the graves of over 25,000 soldiers and has eight marble courts bearing the names of those missing in action from WWII, the Korean War and the Vietnam War.

112-113 Orderly rows of houses line up at the base of Diamond Head, a place sacred to the ancient Hawaiians and the unmistakable symbol of Oahu. The highest rim of the crater is at 758 feet and offers excellent panoramic views.

113 top and center At the easternmost end of the upwind coast, the strange little island of Mànana emerges. Today a bird sanctuary, in the past this tuffaceous cone accommodated a rabbit breeding farm, from which it got its other name: Rabbit Island.

113 bottom The meager vegetation of this emergence off Waimanalo Beach is emblematic of the evolution of the Hawaiian Islands. Forged by fire and born of the sea, devoid of any form of life, over the millennia the islands became accidentally populated by wave-, wind, or bird-borne biological colonizers. The possibilities for surviving such a crossing are obviously slim.

OAHU

114-115 Kailua,
the Hawaiian
Islands second most
extensive city,
extends in orderly
loops at the foot of
the Koolau
Mountains, which
separate it from
Honolulu.

115 top, top center,
and bottom center
Brilliant as
turquoise, wide
Kailua Bay
embraces the beach
of the same name,
pleasantly wide and
quiet.

115 bottom A
succession of waves
sluices toward the
sand of Waimanalo
Beach, just south of
Kailua Bay. The
beach offers four
miles of relaxing
emptiness.

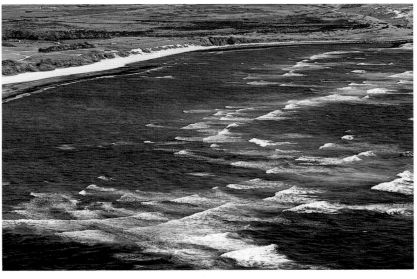

One of the walls of the Koko Head Crater fell away about 6,000 years ago, causing a rush of ocean water to flood in, creating Hanauma Bay. A coral reef stretches across the mouth of the bay separating the shallow waters from the ocean resulting in a sort of natural aquarium. Waikiki Beach is remembered in Hawaiian history as the place where legend states that King Kamehameha the Great ordered human sacrifices to

the gods following his conquest of Oahu in 1795. The legend states that this was where, in 1804, he assembled his army of 7,000 warriors to attack the island of Kauai, the last bastion of the Hawaiian Islands to succumb to his rule. (The attack never occurred and Kauai later joined the unified kingdom voluntarily.)

At the opposite end of the island, the North Shore from Laie to Ka'ena Point is world famous for its death-defying waves that carry only the bravest and most skilled of surfers. The winter surf here can bring in 30-foot rollers, and rogue waves even make walking along the beach dangerous! Waimea Valley, north-east, is famed for its 50-foot waterfall and its 250-foot bluff overlooking the entire North Shore where the *kahuna* (priests) had a sacred temple and made human sacrifices—two or three of whom were captives taken from Captain George Vancouver's ship, HMS *Daedalus*, in 1792. Today the site is a park with reportedly 6,000 varieties of plants, many rare and endangered, and 25 of the 30 varieties of banana (at one time there were 50). Ka'ena Point is also now protected as a conservation area. Continuing from Ka'ena Point along the coastline all the way to

Makapu'u Point is the windward coast of the island, flanked by the Koolau Mountains that making the coast popular with hang gliders because of the abundant thermals and brilliant views. If the visitor doesn't have the luxury of a sky-high perspective, then Nuuanu Pali Lookout grants excellent views, one of which is the panorama of Waimanalo Beach. This is Oahu's longest strip of sand; extending for almost four miles, it snakes along the bay like an elegant ribbon between the water and the mountains. The stunning coastal vistas that visitors to Makapu'u Point can enjoy include Makapu'u Beach, a favorite spot for surfers; Kailua, where Kamehameha the Great defeated the defenders of Oahu and ran them off the cliffs; Sandy Beach, the island's most dangerous because of rip currents and shore-pounding breakers; and finally Koko Head Crater. The Makapu'u lighthouse, which was once manned but is now automated, stands at the tip of Makapu'u Point, still reliably sending its beacon light out across the ocean. At the southeasternmost point there is a lookout for spotting humpback whales (*Megaptera novaeangliae*), which can be seen offshore between November and April. Also in this area is Halona Blowhole, an old lava tube that is a spectacular sight, throwing skyward great plumes of seawater, sometimes up to 50 feet high. The more subdued Halona Cove is frequented by green sea turtles (*Chelonia mydas*).

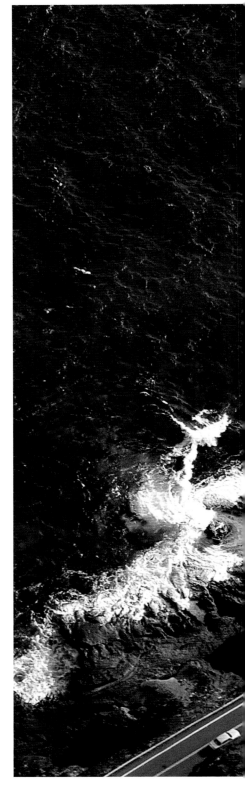

116 Only 46 feet
high, the lighthouse
at Makapuu Point is
of vital assistance to
ships approaching
Honolulu from the
American west
coast. Its light-beam
is visible from 28
miles away.

117 top An ancient
volcanic cone half
underwater and
eroded on the
seaward side, the
Manauma Bay
amphitheater
protects waters full
of life, favored by a
light, warm current
in its shallower
parts.

116-117
A two-lane roads
runs along almost
the entire perimeter
of Oahu. Starting
at Honolulu,
Highway 1 passes
through Makapuu

Point, on the
northernmost end of
the island, and
continues until
Haleiwa, where the
rugged coastline
forces it to deviate
inland.

118 top and center West of the Mokapu Peninsula, Kaneohe Bay opens out, lined by residential areas and home to the University of Hawaii's Marine Biology Laboratory.

118 bottom The epitome of tropical seas, Hanauma Bay is all that remains of a volcanic crater invaded by the ocean, forming a protected area for fish.

119 top A small dock extends out from Kaneohe Bay.

118-119 Beyond the white spots on the deep bottom of Kaneohe Bay, the edges of one of the island's three oldest fish pens can be traced. This technique an ahead-of-its-time aquaculture, since the captured fish were raised in a "controlled" marine environment.

120 and 121 The boundary between deep water and the shallows creates a very fine veil of hues just beyond the shoreline. At low tide, some sandbars are under only 4 to 6 feet of water. Thus weather forecasts include a table noting the tide's likely ebb and flow and near-shore water depths

122-123 Oahu, the capital island, projects the character of present-day Hawaii: natural beauty and tradition, filtered through an alluring contemporary look.

KAUAI

124-125 Kauai's northern face is its most impressive: Na Pali Coast, a bastion of primordial lava a magnificently frightening look.

125 top left Standing 213 feet above water level, the Kilauea Point lighthouse looks down on the surf off Kauai's northernmost point. The building is a national monument.

125 top and bottom right Haena State Park, east of Na Pali Coast, protects a coastal tract of great beauty, full of caves and subject to a powerful undertow.

Kauai is the oldest of the Hawaiian archipelago's major islands. It was created by a single massive volcano that became extinct approximately six million years ago. A mere 33 miles long by 25 miles wide and with a total area of 533 square miles, Kauai was the only island that Kamehameha the Great did not conquer; it was also the first island that Captain Cook discovered.

Captain James Cook, in command of HMS *Resolution* and HMS *Discovery*, arrived on the shores of Kauai on the eve of January 20, 1778. Not recognizing that the island's original discov-

one of rapid extinction not only plants and animals but of practically all of the native people as well. It is believed that in first century following European contact, some 90 percent of all Hawaiians died from diseases brought over from Europe and Asia, against which they had no immunity. As well as disease, the ships that first came to the islands brought hard liquor, guns and other weapons, and furs and tobacco. These had negative impacts on the indigenous culture. Similarly, imported agricultural products and grazing animals wreaked havoc on the native vegetation, while an insatiable greed for aromatic Hawaiian sandal-

erers and current inhabitants had already named Kauai and its sister islands had already named them, Cook announced his 'discovery' of the Sandwich Islands. He named them thus in honor of his patron, the Earl of Sandwich, a lord of the Admiralty. The rate of change on the islands accelerated markedly from the gentle pace of the previous centuries to

wood caused it to be harvested to extinction. At the same time, rats, dogs, cats and other animals made their glorious debut as the islands' first significant predators.

Hurricanes are among other assaults that Kauai has endured; in fact the island seems particularly susceptible to them. In the last century alone, three major windstorms have struck this tiny

KAUAI

126

island. Hurricane Iniki, the most recent one, hit on September 11, 1992. Before the wind meters broke they clocked wind-speeds of 227 miles per hour, with the furious force leaving nary a leaf on a tree and damaging or destroying 70 percent of all the island's homes. Most of Kauai no longer shows any sign of this damage, but some remnants of

the storm are still visible along the Coconut Coast. The Coast made a comeback and remains one of the island's most popular vacation areas. It is proud of its large stand of coconut palms, planted in the mid-1800s and still standing.

Despite all these ordeals—its early discovery, frequent natural disasters, and being the oldest of

the islands—most of Kauai remains pristine, rural and undeveloped, with most of the natural areas protected by their designation as nature reserves and parks. With the exception of Lihue (the one major city), restrictions on construction have prevented most buildings from being built higher than a coconut palm. Instead, skyscraping emer-

ald peaks form Kauai's skyline, one that runs from center to shore, formed by the architecture of nature that has been at work on this island for millions of years. Her tools were lava, wind, rain and waves ... and perhaps a little help from the mythological *Menehune*, who were masters of engineering and construction.

128-129 Liuhu Harbor is the island's county seat, a lovely town that is the arrival point for visitors to Kauai.

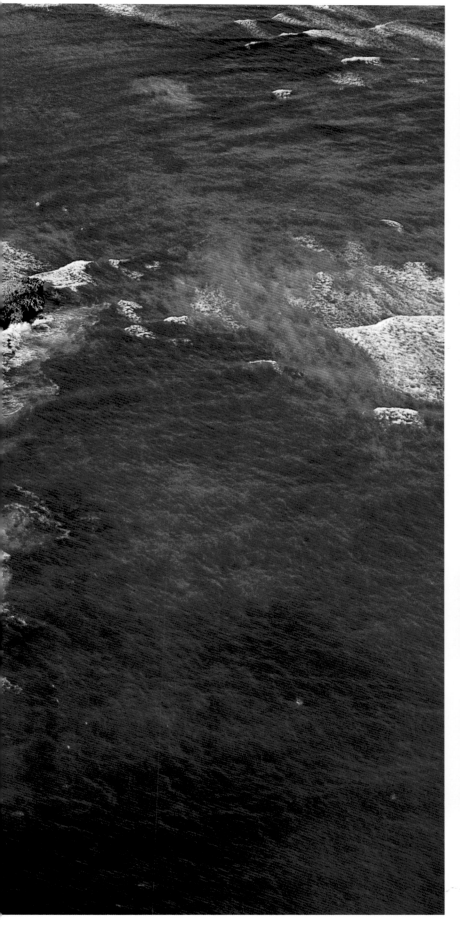

130-131 The relaxing green of taro fields, kalo loi, introduces visitors to Hanalei Valley, a series of valleys of great beauty that, as a nature reserve, are partly closed to the public. This is no problem for birdwatchers; protected species often wander onto the farms.

132-133 Amid a network of agrarian boundaries, the cone of Puu Hunihuni stands at the base of the island's "father," the great volcano Wai'ale'ale.

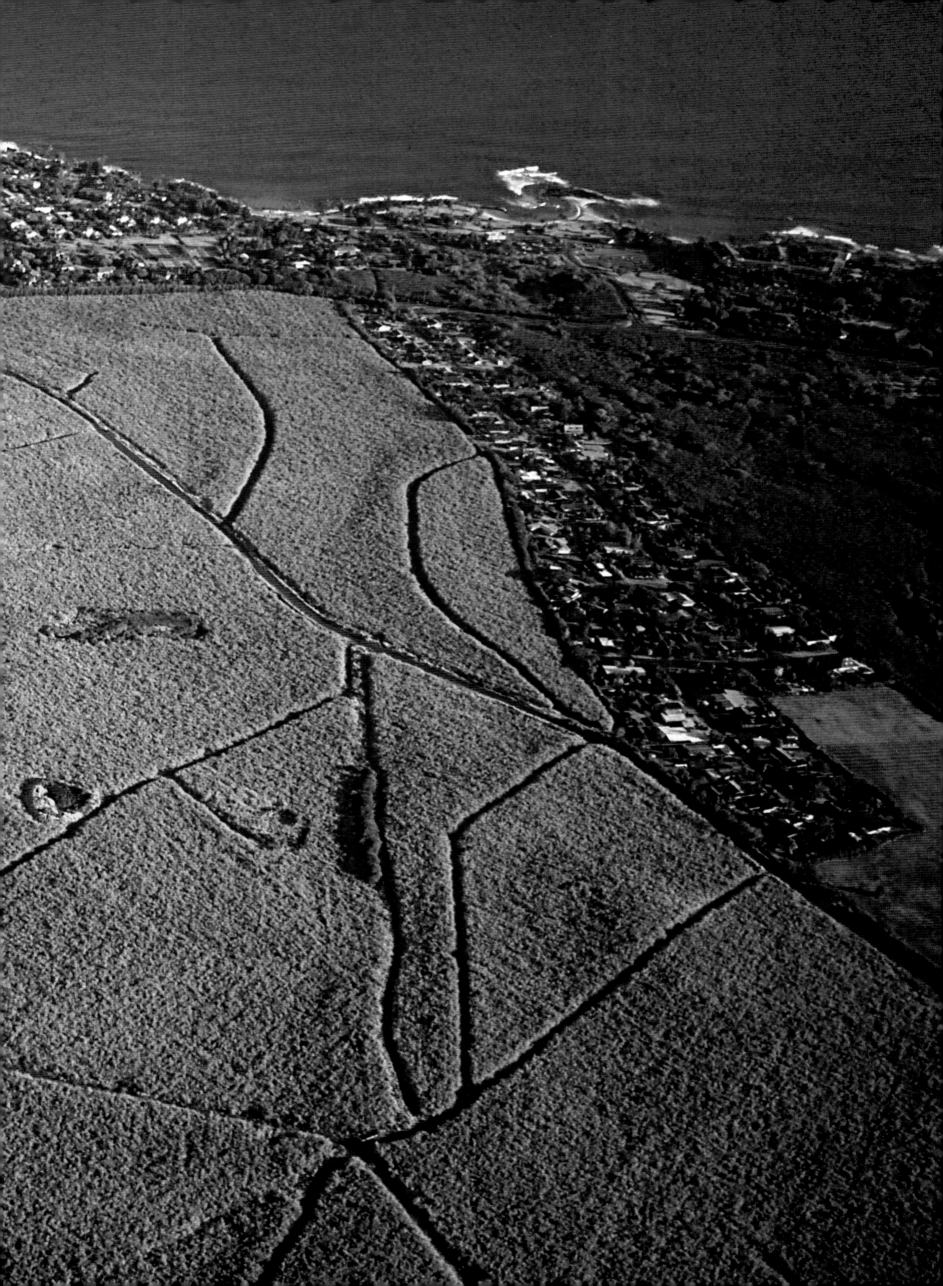

Kauai is the legendary home of these leprechaun-like people. By whatever means, Kauai took on a stunning and unique form. Kauai's distinct geographic diversity is highlighted by jagged mountain ranges that end abruptly at the ocean in dramatic sea cliffs etched with caves and ravines and by arid desert landscapes that contrast with tropical forests and great surging, yet often navigable rivers. Nor should the 43 sandy beaches that wrap around the island like a lei be forgotten.

The greater part of Kauai's remote, mountainous interior can be seen only from a helicopter or plane. Rising more than 5,000 feet from the middle of the island are its highest peaks, Mount Wai'ale'ale (5,148 feet) and Mount Kawaikini (5,243 feet). Wai'ale'ale has the distinction of being one of the world's wettest places, gathering more than 40 feet of rain a year. Narrow waterfalls burst and stream from Wai'ale'ale's countless rain-forest-clad cliffs, and ferns and flowers scramble atop each other reaching and poking out of the moist rainforest canopy. Much of Wai'ale'ale and Kawaikini is protected in largely inaccessible forest reserves. Native flora and fauna, such as rare Hawaiian honeycreepers (*Palmeria* spp.), fight extinction in these remote sanctuaries. The honeycreeper is one of the most amazing examples of island evolution. When Darwin studied his famous finches of the Galapagos, science was astonished to learn of 12 genetic variations of the species resulting from small populations being geographically isolated from each other and evolving independently. The honeycreeper of the Hawaiian Islands diverged and has evolved into 57 distinctly separate variants of the species!

In Kauai's earliest formative years, a colossal earthquake practically ripped the island in half causing all the mountain streams to divert toward the

134 Deep folds wrinkle the seawall of Na Pali Coast, dug out by the force of nature over six million years. Na Pali simply means "the sea cliffs" in the Hawaiian language.

135 Admiring Na Pali, it seems impossible that humans ever lived and prospered there, and yet this area, as magnificent as it is impenetrable, was populated from the 9th century B.C. until 1919.

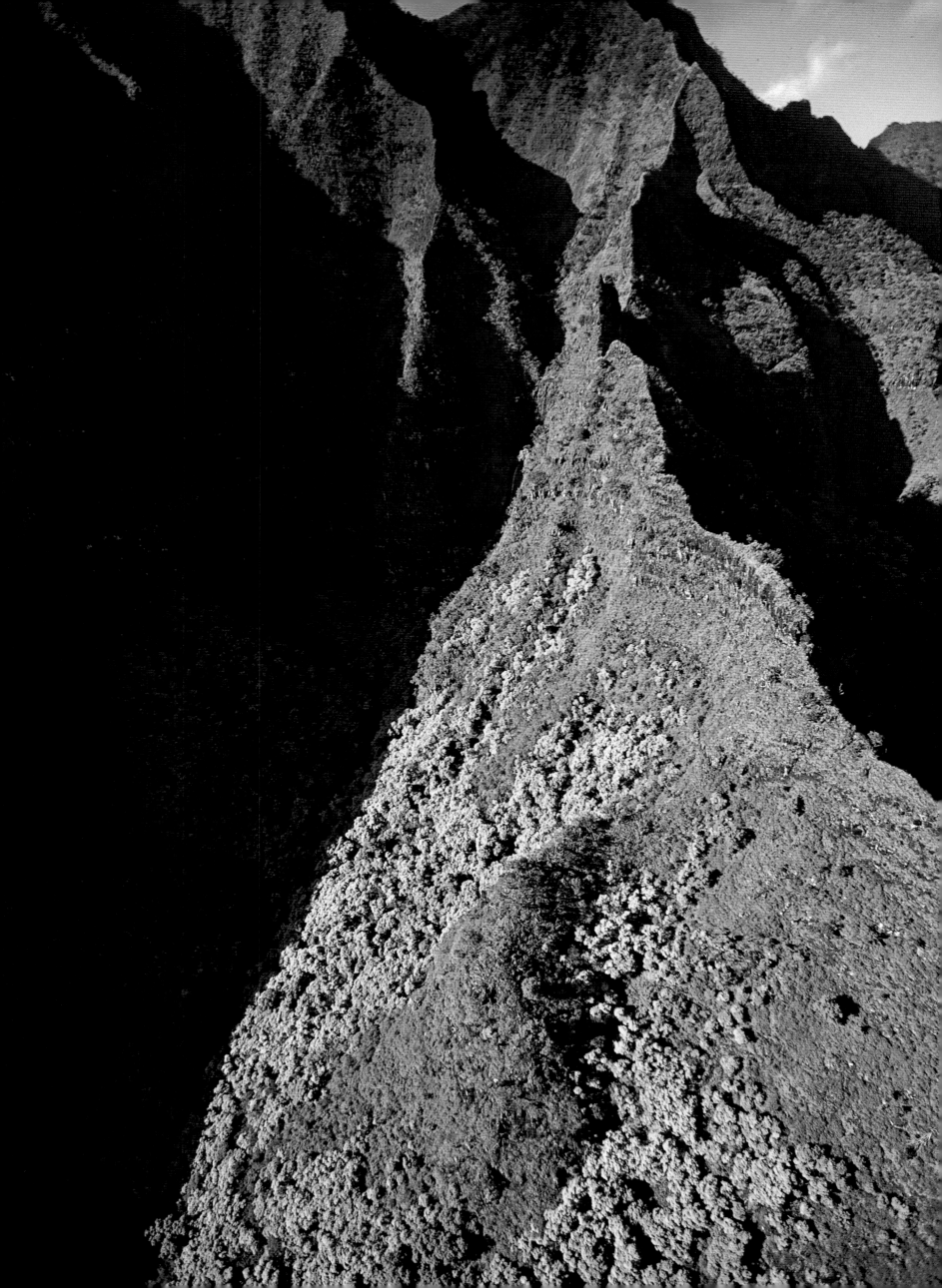

fault into one massive swollen river. Centuries of erosion from the driving waters of the powerful Waimea River wore away at the ravine forming the massive and awesome Waimea Canyon, the largest in the Pacific. Mark Twain described this 14-mile long, 3,600-foot-deep gorge as the "Grand Canyon of the Pacific." To fly above the canyon is breathtaking. The immense grandeur of the rugged and sculpted landscape is awash with a multitude of colors, greens, reds, purples, and grays contrasting with the bright sunlit rocky peaks and lush foliage against the shadows and contours of the deep valleys and ravines.

Kokee State Park is 4,354 acres of cloud forest high above Waimea Canyon and overlooking the Napali Coast. New species of plant and animal are still being discovered throughout this pristine area. The Alakai Swamp covers the floor of the volcanic caldera, 13 miles in diameter and 4,000 feet above sea level. It holds the source waters of all the rivers on Kauai and is credited as being the wettest place in the world. Passing these soggy heights, the last of the jagged cliffs drops from 2,000 feet down to the sapphire sea and secluded golden beaches of the isolated Na Pali Coast. No roads scar this shoreline of sacred, deep green valleys surrounded by majestic mountains and cathedral cliffs. This enchanted coastline is where the mythical Menehune once made

their mischief; sometimes one can almost swear to have caught a glimpse of one of these wee folk behind the cascading curtain of a waterfall or peeking from deep within the dark impenetrable foliage. The wild mystique of the Na Pali Coast allows the imagination to float off in magical directions and brings a feeling of slipping back to the time of the ancients.

The towering cliffs of the Na Pali Coast frame one side of the beautiful Hanalei Bay, which is flanked on the other side by the Hanalei River. The river flows through the valley and floods the emerald-green *kalo loi* (taro) fields. Between the cliffs and the river, a two-mile-long beach of white sand stretches along the bay and can be seen from the air

to curve like a smile. Beyond the beach are thousand-foot cliffs with rainbow-laden waterfalls. The three villages of Hanalei, Wainiha and Haena are tucked away in the foliage.

The 200 acres of Kilauea Point National Wildlife Refuge lie at the northernmost tip of Kauai and atop the 216-foot, wave-lashed cliff on which the ancient Hawaiians used to hold night-watch parties to tend the *kukui ahi*, fires that guided fishermen home. Today the Kilauea Point lighthouse mans the lookout. This 52-foot white tower houses the world's largest clamshell lens, capable of projecting its beam 90 miles out to sea.

Sugarcane and pineapples have been under cultivation

since the early Polynesians first introduced them to the island's hospitable climes. They grew the plants only for personal consumption; early immigrants to Hawaii began cultivation on a commercial scale and then marketed the harvest. In 1813, pineapples were brought from Spain and a successful pineapple plantation was established in 1835, at Koloa, Kauai. By 1900 sugar cane was successfully introduced on Kauai's mineral-rich volcanic soil and soon became this island's primary industry, closely followed by the pineapple. The budding sugar and pineapple industries, blessed with of rain and stable temperatures and offering the possibility of major profits, soon caught the attention of enterprising American entrepreneurs. The most noteworthy of them was James Dole, who began canning pineapple chunks on a mass scale in the first years of the 1900s. Private ownership of land was relatively unknown to the native Hawaiians, but once the Americans began to arrive and claim large sections of land for their plantations and mills, Western concepts of land ownership were implemented. As a result, many locals were pushed off areas they cultivated or lived on. Kauai's last sugar cane plantation, one of only two left in the state, is owned and operated by the Gay Robinson family, which owns 51,000 acres on Kauai and all of Niihau, a small, low-lying island 17 miles off Kauai's western shore.

136 Silver threads weave through the velvety vegetation on the crags of Kauai. The volcano Wai'ale'ale, the highest point on the island, holds the record as the most humid spot on earth.

137 top and bottom Waimea Canyon upholds the expectation of magnificence first hinted at by Na Pali: this universe of steep and luxuriant rock faces is breathtaking.

138 top Waimea Canyon is the kingdom of light and shadow. The sun molds an incomparably beautiful panorama, ever creating new sources of fascination.

138 bottom A series of four gorges form the area of Waimea Canyon, in which three secondary branches crisscross for 14 miles.

138-139 Mark Twain's description of Waimea Canyon fully fits the area: "the Grand Canyon of the Pacific" makes visitors feel no less small than does its larger cousin.

140 *Natural erosion caused by wind and abundant rains (the actual cause of Waimea Canyon's existence), has stripped vast areas of ground of most vegetation. The environment must* nonetheless be *"maintained" by teams of professionals and volunteers who uproot weeds and block the expansion of landslides to contain the loss of land.*

140-141 *Toward the top of the valley, the view ranges over plateaus from which the Waimea River sculpted this wonder of the natural world. The system of gorges probably had its origin in an earthquake.*

142-143 *Like a cameo, the eroded land changes color according to the layers bared by the weather.*

*144 top and bottom
The island's red soil,
according to the
quality of the clay,
lime, and sand, is
fantastic for
farming, which
above all means the
cultivation of sugar
cane on Kauai.*

*144-145
The traditional
organization of
territory for its
exploitation (used in
Hawaii for centuries
before Western
colonists arrived)
was based on the
division of the land
into vertical*

*"slices." The ran
from the top of the
highlands to below
sea level, thus
including all
elements of the
changing
environment,
such as lakes,
waterways, plants,
and animals.*

146-147 Heavy vehicles till the sugar cane fields for the new planting season. Sugar-cane cultivation, which was soon produced Hawaii's most important export commodity, became successful on Kauai in the first half of the 1800s.

146 top and 147 top and bottom right Ochre-colored land rings the plantation sections that dominate Kauai's rural landscape.

148-149 An open amphitheater on the vast ocean, the Kalalau Valley, located exactly north of the Waimea Canyon, descends steeply toward Na Pali Coast.

*150-151
The curtains of the
northern spurs of
Kauai stretch
uninterruptedly
northeast for 16
miles before the
coast flattens out
again, in the area of
Kee Beach Park.*

*151 top The sharp
spires honed by the
rain tell the island's
history, laying bare
the structure of
Wai'ale'ale, which
at 5050 feet
dominates the coast.*

*151 bottom Along
the last tract in the
direction of its
easternmost end, the
northern coast of
Kawai becomes
absolutely
impassable on foot.*

152 top and bottom
Perpetually crowned
by white wave-crests,
Kee Beach Park's lush
panorama marks the
Na Pali Coast's
eastern end. The
Park's magnificent
coral gardens
welcome airborne
visitors.

152-153 The
environmental
variety on Kauai
depends on the
climatic zone along
the slopes of
Wai'ale'ale, where
the temperature can
range from 86°F to
48°F.

154-155 From a
human perspective,
Kauai exists within
a dramatic clash of
the elements: there
is a lack of balance,
but the result is
sense of unity.

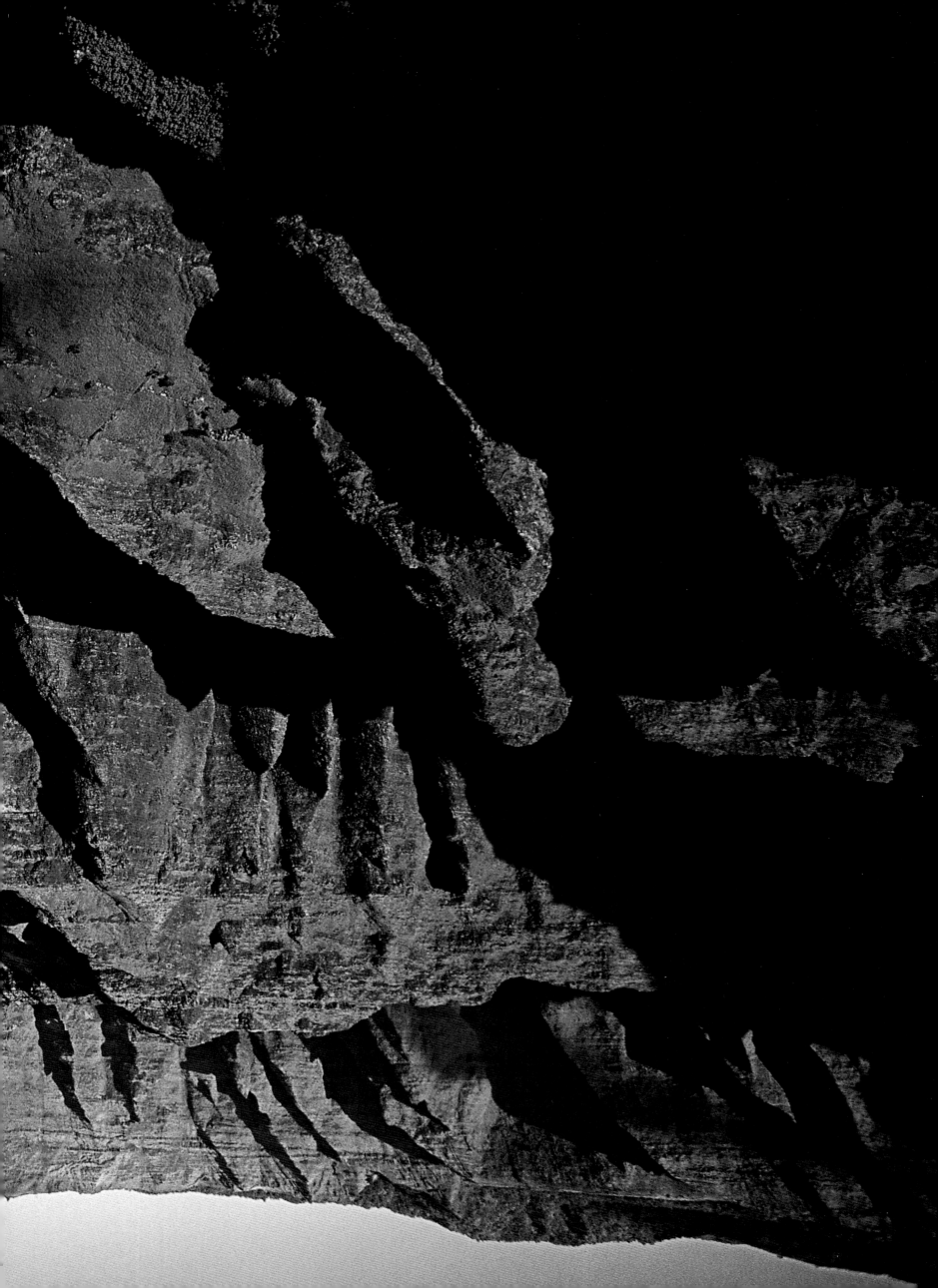

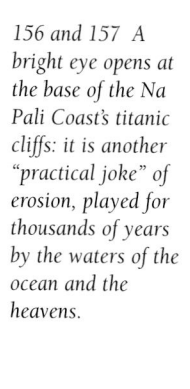

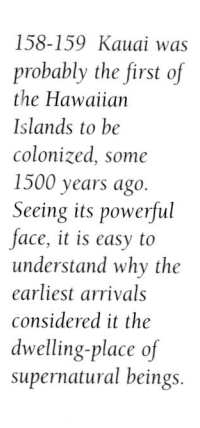

156 and 157 A bright eye opens at the base of the Na Pali Coast's titanic cliffs: it is another "practical joke" of erosion, played for thousands of years by the waters of the ocean and the heavens.

158-159 Kauai was probably the first of the Hawaiian Islands to be colonized, some 1500 years ago. Seeing its powerful face, it is easy to understand why the earliest arrivals considered it the dwelling-place of supernatural beings.

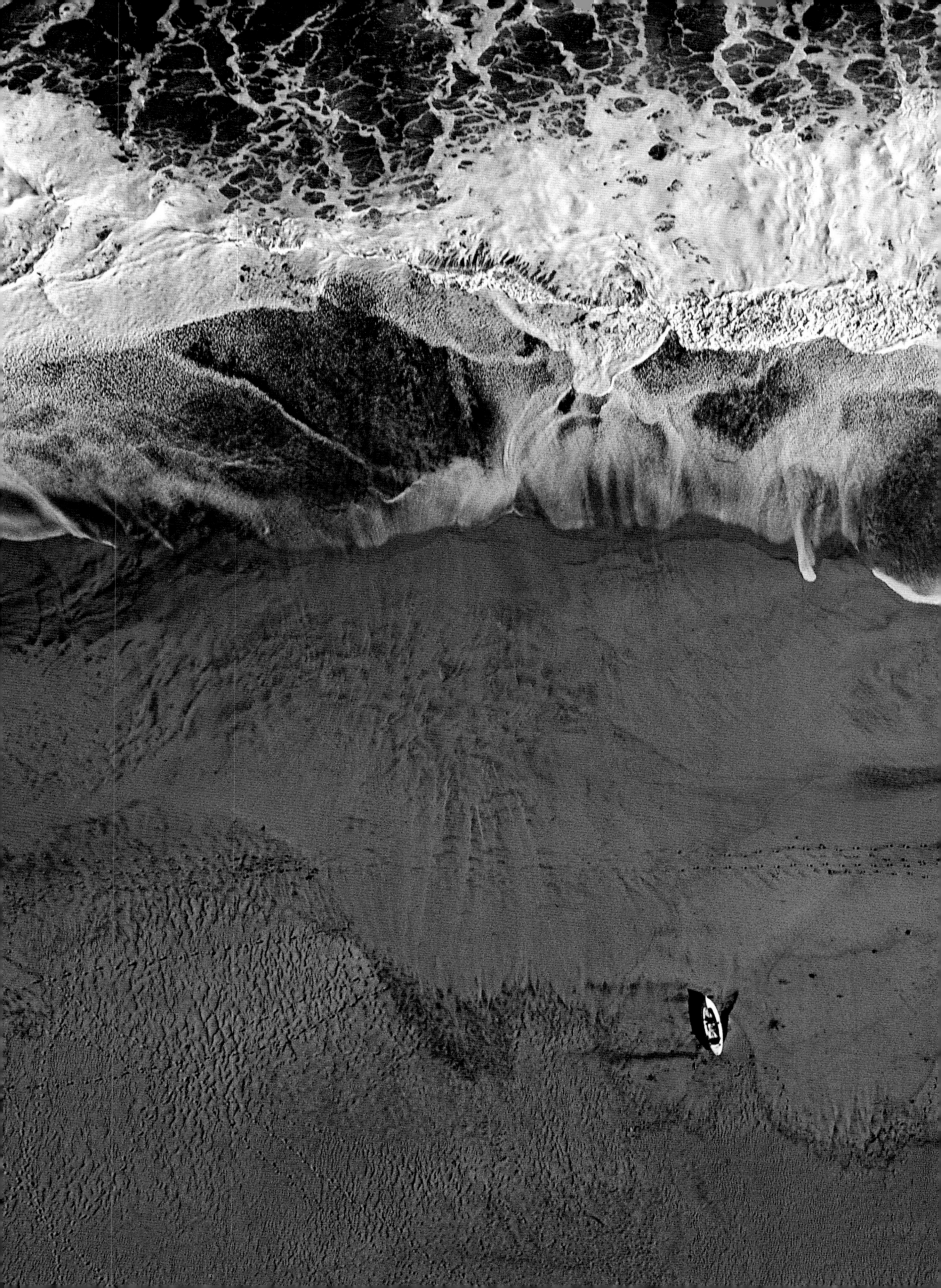

160 Unbelievable peaks, a sea deeper than one wishes to fathom, and veils of rare vegetation as soft as velvet: with its embrace of lava rock, Kaiaupapa Coast, on Molokai, shines with all the beauty the Hawaiian Islands offer.

PHOTO CREDITS

All the pictures inside the book are by Antonio Attini except for the following: